Language Rights and the Law in the United States and Its Territories

Language Rights and the Law in the United States and Its Territories

Eduardo D. Faingold

LEXINGTON BOOKS
Lanham • Boulder • New York • London

Published by Lexington Books
An imprint of The Rowman & Littlefield Publishing Group, Inc.
4501 Forbes Boulevard, Suite 200, Lanham, Maryland 20706
www.rowman.com

6 Tinworth Street, London SE11 5AL

British Library Cataloguing in Publication Information Available

Library of Congress Cataloging-in-Publication Data

Names: Faingold, Eduard D., author
Title: Language rights and the law in the United States and its territories / Eduardo Faingold.
Description: Lanham, Md. : Lexington Books, 2018. | Includes bibliographical references and index.
Identifiers: LCCN 2018040852 (print) | LCCN 2018041242 (ebook) | ISBN 9781498571371 (electronic) | ISBN 9781498571364 (cloth : alk. paper)
Subjects: LCSH: Linguistic rights—United States. | Minorities—Legal status, laws, etc.—United States. | Language and languages—Political aspects—United States.
Classification: LCC KF4755 (ebook) | LCCKF4755 .F35 2018 (print) | DDC 342.7308/5—dc23
LC record available at https://lccn.loc.gov/2018040852

∞™ The paper used in this publication meets the minimum requirements of American National Standard for Information Sciences Permanence of Paper for Printed Library Materials, ANSI/NISO Z39.48-1992.

Printed in the United States of America

In memory of my father,
ENRIQUE FAINGOLD
(1925-2012)

Contents

Contents

Preface

Language issues have been of importance to the national identity of the United States for a long time (Ricento, 1996). The United States as a nation, the fifty states, and the United States island territories of the Caribbean and the Pacific all have recognizable interests and ways of dealing with language questions. In this book, I examine some of the U.S. federal, state, and territorial laws pertaining to the language rights of the inhabitants of the United States and its territories.

This work began as a side project that entailed a critical contemplation of the language rights of individuals and groups in the constitutions of the world (Faingold, 2004a) and the 2004 draft of the European Union constitution (Faingold, 2007) more than a decade ago. Throughout my academic career, my professional fields of research and interest have included bilingualism, psycholinguistics, sociolinguistics, historical linguistics, and the biographical study of immigrants and exiles. Where the topic of language rights in the United States, where I have lived for nearly three decades, was concerned, I had to rely on my own observations of the American political scene and on reading newspapers, magazines, and the works of scholars and activists. I felt that I was standing on shaky ground. Mostly because the evidence in the scholarly literature seemed to be often erroneous (e.g., Kymlicka's [1995] claim that the Treaty of Guadalupe Hidalgo protects the language rights of Hispanics in the Southwest) or based on ideology rather than fact (e.g., King's [1997, 1999] assertion that one should always leave language alone, rather than enact legislation to solve linguistic conflicts). That is why, to satisfy my curiosity, in the early 2010s, I decided to embark on the study of language rights and the law in the United States and its territories. The project would eventually include analyzing the U.S. Constitution and the Civil Rights Act of 1964, the constitutions of the fifty states, the organic acts, constitutions, and statutes of all of the U.S. territories (i.e., Puerto Rico, the United States Virgin Islands, Guam, the Commonwealth of the Northern Mariana Islands, and American Samoa) and the Freely Associated States (i.e., the Federated States of Micronesia, the Republic of the Marshall Islands, and the Republic of Palau), and producing detailed case studies of language legislation in the Southwestern states, where Spanish-speakers live in large numbers, as well as case studies of linguistic minorities in the U.S. Pacific island territories of Guam and the Commonwealth of the Northern Mariana Islands (i.e., Chamorro and Carolinian).

Earlier versions of some of the chapters in this book appeared in the journal *Language Problems and Language Planning* (chapters 1, 2, and 7), published by John Benjamins, and the book series *Readings in Language Studies* (chapters 3, 4, and 5), published by the International Society for Language Studies. Permission to use these articles in this book are properly acknowledged in the acknowledgments section.

I have extensively revised and updated previously published research (chapters 1, 2, 3, 4, 5, and 7), to account for changes in the legal systems of U.S. states and territories from 2010 to 2017 (e.g., the passing of Proposition 58 in 2016, which restored bilingual education in California's public schools; the passing of HB 3019 in 2016, which required that all official state business in West Virginia be conducted in English) and to account for changes in my thinking (e.g., the rejection of King's [1997, 1999] views on language policy, that one should always leave language alone; the use of language devolution as a framework to create positive change in the field of language rights). Some arguments were made more clear or concise, while others were expanded. A number of errors were corrected, including a few misclassifications and minor mistakes. Four completely new chapters were written especially for this book (introduction and chapters 6, 8, and 9).

Revisions to chapter 1 have benefited from comments by Prof. Daniel Villa and the audience at the 19th International Congress of Linguists, Geneva, Switzerland, July 2013.

Revisions to chapter 3 have benefitted from comments by the audiences at the Annual Meeting of the Society of Oklahoma Linguists, Oklahoma City, March 2007, the Sociolinguistics Symposium 17, Amsterdam, April 2008, and the International Society for Language Studies, Aruba, June 2011.

Revisions to chapter 4 have benefited from comments by audiences at the 4th Annual Symposium of the John Hope Franklin Center for Reconciliation, Tulsa, Oklahoma, May 2013, Multidisciplinary Approaches in Language Policy and Planning Conference, Calgary, Canada, September 2013, and the Conference of the International Society for Language Studies, Albuquerque, New Mexico, June 2015.

Revisions to chapter 5 have benefited from comments by audiences at the 40th Annual meeting of the Linguistics Association of the Southwest, Brownsville, Texas, October 2011, and the International Society for Language Studies, San Juan, Puerto Rico, June 2013.

Revisions to chapter 6 have benefited from comments by audiences at the 24th Conference on Spanish in the United States and Spanish in Contact with other Languages, McAllen, Texas, March 2013, Communication in the "Country of Babel": Language Ideological Debates on Contact Varieties, Bern, Switzerland, November 2015, and the International Society for Language Studies, Honolulu, Hawaii, June 2017.

Revisions to chapter 7 have benefited from comments by the audience at the conference Exploring Language Education: Global and Local Perspectives, Stockholm, Sweden, June 2018.

Acknowledgments

I am grateful to Prof. Lani Guinier, Harvard Law School, for her advice to approach the laws of the United States critically when dealing with issues concerning minorities, and to Bishop Samuel Ruiz, formerly of Chiapas, Mexico, for challenging me to use my knowledge of linguistics for the benefit of minorities, during my tenure as a fellow of the Salzburg Seminar, Schloss Leopoldskron, Salzburg, Austria, 1999, Session 372, Race and Ethnicity: Social Change through Public Awareness. I am grateful also to Prof. Dr. Armin von Bogdandy, Director of the Max Planck Institute for Comparative Public Law and International Law in Heidelberg, Germany, for an invitation to do research at his institute in 2014, where the idea for this book was conceived.

Chapter 1 originally appeared in *Language Problems and Language Planning,* volume 36: 2 (2012), pp. 136–148. © John Benjamins Publishing Company. Reprinted with permission.

Chapter 2 originally appeared in *Language Problems and Language Planning,* volume 41: 2 (2017), pp. 103–114. © John Benjamins Publishing Company. Reprinted with permission.

Chapter 3 originally appeared in Miller, P. C., Watzke, J. L., & Mantero, M. (Eds.). (2012). *Readings in Language Studies, Volume 3: Language and Identity* (pp. 447–457). © International Society for Language Studies. Reprinted with permission.

Chapter 4 originally appeared in Miller, P. C., Rubrecht, B., Mikulec, E., & McGivern, C. T. (Eds.), (2016). *Readings in Language Studies, Volume 6: A Critical Examination of Language and Community* (pp. 1–13). © International Society for Language Studies. Reprinted with permission.

Chapter 5 originally appeared in Miller, P. C., Watzke, J. L., & Mantero, M. (Eds.). (2014). *Readings in Language Studies, Volume 4: Language and Social Justice* (pp. 271–281). © International Society for Language Studies. Reprinted with permission.

Chapter 7 originally appeared in *Language Problems and Language Planning,* volume 42: 2 (2018), pp. 113–131. © John Benjamins Publishing Company. Reprinted with permission.

I am indebted to the Office of the Dean of Arts and Sciences at the University of Tulsa and the W. K. Kellogg Foundation for grants to travel to Salzburg, Austria, to attend Session 372 of the Salzburg Seminar in the fall of 1999, where my interest in language rights was piqued for the first time. This research was supported in part by seven University of Tulsa Faculty Research Grants in 2003, 2010, 2013 (twice), 2014, 2015, and 2016 (#20–2–1010130).

Introduction

In many regions of the world languages coexist uneasily. Whether real or apparent, a dominant-dominated relationship exists between speakers of many majority and minority languages. The drafting of explicit language legislation, especially in a constitution, highlights the existence of conflicts among languages coexisting within the same nation. Ideally the purpose of language legislation should be to solve such conflicts by legally defining the status and use of coexisting languages (Faingold, 2004a; Tully, 1995; Turi, 1994). One or more languages can be targeted for promotion and development through the drafting of explicit language legislation that specifies both language rights for individuals and groups and language obligations by the nation according to law. In practice, however, language legislation is sometimes used to enshrine the dominant rights of one language group over another, rather than to solve conflicts among speakers (Faingold, 2007, 2015, 2016b). One example of explicit language legislation is Title 7, Sections 16-22, of the Canadian Constitution, which specifies the right to public instruction of speakers of the two official languages of Canada, English and French (Burnaby, 1996; Mackey, 2010; MacMillan, 1998). Another example is the post-apartheid constitution of the Republic of South Africa, which came into effect in May 1994, in which eleven languages are listed as having official status nationally, and many other languages, in addition to the official languages, are promoted for development and use (Alexander, 2004; du Plessis, 2000; Reagan, 2004). In contrast, such diverse nations as the United States, Uruguay, Japan, and the Netherlands have no explicit language legislation nor do they promulgate any official languages in their national constitutions. This, of course, does not mean that these nations have no implicit language policies that promote the languages of the majority (e.g., English in the United States; see Phillipson & Skutnabb-Kangas, 1996; Ricento, 1996; Shohamy, 2006).

This book analyzes the language policies that result from the promulgation of linguistic rights in the constitutions, organic acts, and statutes of the United States and its territories. The United States is a nation in which speakers of minority languages were conquered or incorporated and the languages spoken by them were suppressed or neglected. Since the 1960s, the United States and its territories have seen a resurgence of claims for language recognition by minority groups representing a considerable population (e.g., Spanish in Puerto Rico, the United States Virgin Islands, and the Southwestern states, Chamorro in Guam, Chamorro and Carolinian in the Northern Mariana Islands, and Samoan in American Samoa). Also, the book examines recent developments regarding the status and use of English in the United States and its territories. For example, studying the effects of legal, social, educational, and political contexts on the Spanish language as spoken by Hispanics in the Southwestern states, and Pacific languages (i.e., Chamorro and Carolinian) in Guam and the Northern Mariana Islands, reveals that English continues to be used as the main language of communication in all these places, despite continuous efforts to protect the rights of indigenous languages by their native populations. However, the United States as a nation, nineteen states, and at least one territory of the United States (i.e., the United States Virgin Island), do not mention any languages rights, and do not establish any official languages or provisions to protect the use of English, in their constitutions and/or statutes. For these reasons, it is important to compare the linguistic laws promulgated in the constitutions, organic acts, and statutes of the United States and its territories, or the lack thereof, as a response to the demands for linguistic rights by sectors of the population who do not speak English as a first language or who may seek to maintain the use of one or more minority languages.

The point of this study is to look beyond one single case and to learn of other ways of handling important language policy issues. In presenting these case studies together, the book aims to facilitate not only the understanding and improvement of implicit and explicit language policies, such as the legislation and planning of bilingual acquisition and education and linguistic corpora (e.g., dictionaries, grammars, school curricula, standards for broadcasting, the language of journals and newspapers, bills, laws, etc.) but also the access to comparable information for the development of new theoretical perspectives about the operation of languages in the legal, social, educational, and political contexts. Finally, the book offers insights for the benefit of those in charge of drafting legislation in the area of language rights. It shows how the United States and its territories could recognize and accommodate linguistic diversity.

The introduction presents the issues, themes, and goals of the book, and provides an outline of the chapters in the book.

Chapter 1 studies the constitutions and statutes of the fifty states in the United States. In it, the fifty states are given an exhaustive screening to identify legal language defining the obligations of the state and language rights of individuals and groups. The chapter shows that in the United States, states adopting a "hands-off" linguistic legislation are consistent with the U.S. Constitution, while states adopting a "hands-on" legislation are in conflict with it, since the U.S. Constitution is silent about official languages. With the exception of California, Hawaii, Louisiana, and New Mexico, which enacted language laws that protect linguistic rights of minorities, states that establish English as the official language, without offering any language protections to linguistic minorities, are deemed to be "nativist" because they seem unfavorable toward speakers of minority languages.

Chapter 2 studies the constitutions, organic acts, and statutes of the territories of the United States and the Freely Associated States. In it, the former and the latter are given an exhaustive screening to identify legal language defining the linguistic obligations of each territory or associated state and the language rights of individuals and groups dwelling within. With the exception of the American Virgin Islands, which do not declare any official languages or language provisions in its constitution and statutes, U.S. territories and associated states are well served by "hands-on" policies that protect the linguistic rights of minority groups. Unlike many states in the United States which declare English as the sole official language and/or enact provisions to protect official English, none of the territories and associated states declares English as the sole official language or establishes provisions that hinder the rights of language minority groups.

Chapter 3 shows that neither the U.S. Constitution nor the Civil Rights Act of 1964 define de jure obligations of the United States toward members of language minorities. It argues that the United States may have to recognize certain language rights of minority groups de jure in the writing of future laws and statutes. The Civil Rights Act of 1964 explicitly focuses on national origin, along with gender and religious minorities for protection against discrimination but fails to target linguistic minorities for protection. A revised civil rights legislation is more likely to help solve language conflicts by defining legally the status of speakers of languages other than English in the United States.

Chapter 4 taps well-established state-of-the-art theories of bilingualism and neurolinguistics as evidence that the use of minority languages at work constitutes an unconscious and automatic linguistic behavior and shows that the most dominant language requires the activation of inhibitory processes in the production of speech in the bilingual brain. Requiring bilinguals to speak a non-native language at all times has a cost, literally, in neurocognitive terms. Also, the chapter uses sociolinguistic theories of bilingualism to demonstrate that for many Hispanic bilingual speakers their first language is a crucial marker of social and cultural identity. Lacking a business necessity, English-only rules in the workplace can constitute a civil rights violation.

Chapter 5 focuses on the Treaty of Guadalupe Hidalgo (1848), which formalized the annexation of the American Southwest, in the aftermath of the Mexican-American War (1846-1848), in which Mexico lost more than half of its territory to the United States. The consensus among scholars of this Treaty is that the language rights of Hispanics in the Southwest are protected by it. This chapter shows that a close reading of the Treaty reveals that it was not designed to protect the linguistic rights of Hispanics in the annexed territories of the Southwest, and that the Treaty is, therefore, not the correct legal instrument to protect the language rights of Hispanics. Stronger legal protections for linguistic minorities can be found in more modern civil rights legislation.

Chapter 6 shows that in the United States, states, cities, and districts may have the power to establish devolution schemes to gain access to bilingual services, bilingual education, and language protections. Under such schemes, Spanish-speakers can receive devolved language rights in congressional districts and cities with the greatest concentration of Hispanics, which are found in the southwestern states of Arizona, California, New Mexico, and Texas, in direct proximity to Mexico. Hispanics in the Southwest, it is claimed, are an indigenous minority group who suffered conquest through armed struggle with a powerful neighbor, the United States, followed by social and economic displacement, while maintaining a separate identity and significantly distinct cultural values, including their own language.

Chapter 7 examines the language legislation of the United States territory of Guam as stated in the Organic Act of Guam (1950) and its legal statutes. As in a few states in the United States (i.e., California, Hawaii, Louisiana, and New Mexico), Guam established language laws with provisions that protect the language rights of its minority, the native Chamorro population of Guam, especially in the areas of education and language standardization (i.e., the production of dictionaries and a standard spelling system). In spite of the impressive array of language laws enacted by Guam's legislature to teach Chamorro language and culture in the schools for more than half a century, the use of English is increasing, while that of Chamorro is continuously shrinking in Guam. The loss of Chamorro appears to be due to a lack of gaining Chamorro indigenous population buy-in of the importance of expanding the use of this language for the purpose of maintaining a modern-day Chamorro identity.

Chapter 8 examines the language legislation of the United States territory of the Northern Mariana Islands in its constitution (1978) and legal statutes. The territory of the Northern Mariana Islands failed to establish any language laws that might protect the language rights of its indigenous population in the schools (i.e., Chamorro and Carolinian), but it enacted constitutional provisions that protect the right to use these languages in the courts. In the Northern Mariana Islands, the use of English is increasing, while the use of its indigenous languages is shrinking, due, it seems, to lack of support for the teaching of Chamorro and Carolinian in the schools by both the legislature and the Board of Education of the Northern Mariana Islands.

Chapter 9 summarizes the findings of the book and offers conclusions and directions for future research for the study of language rights in the U.S. territories.

I

U.S. State, Territorial, and Freely Associated State Language Rights Legislation

ONE

Language Rights in the Fifty States of the United States

The drafting of language legislation highlights the existence of language conflict between majority and minority languages coexisting within a nation. By legally defining the status and use of such languages, language legislation can be used to resolve such conflicts (Faingold, 2004a; Tully 1995; Turi 1994). The legislation typically targets one or more languages for promotion and development if it is *explicit* legislation, which is legislation that specifies both language rights for individuals and groups and also language obligations of the nation according to law (Phillipson, 2003; Phillipson & Skutnabb-Kangas, 1996). Language legislation can be the result of constitutional initiatives, that is, drafting or amending a constitution (Cameron & Krikorian, 2008; Faingold, 2007; Wiseman, 2010), or, more often, the result of a legislative initiative to change the legal statutes of the nation or state without making changes to the nation's or state's constitution (Brown-Blake, 2006; Faingold, 2004a; Garibova & Asgarova, 2009).

In some cases, language legislation is used to enshrine the dominant rights of one language group over another rather than to solve conflicts among speakers (Crawford, 2000; Song, 2011; Varennes, 1996; Zuckerman, 2010). For example, in the United States, the constitutions of the states of Nebraska (1920), Colorado (1988), Florida (1988), Alabama (1990), Arizona (2006), Missouri (2008), and Oklahoma (2010) declare English as the official language of the state and establish language provisions that define the linguistic obligations of the state and citizens to use or develop the official language, without protections for minority languages. Similarly, promulgating nearly identical legislation, but without drafting language laws in their constitutions, the legal statutes of the following states declare English as the official language of the state and define the linguistic obligations of the state and citizens to use or develop the official language, without protections for minority languages: Tennessee (1984); Arkansas, North Carolina, and South Carolina (1987); Montana, New Hampshire, and South Dakota (1995); Georgia, Virginia, and Wyoming (1996); Utah (2000); Iowa (2002); Idaho and Kansas (2007); and West Virginia (2016). In contrast, the constitution of Hawaii (1978) declares both English and Hawaiian as the official languages of Hawaii; the constitution of California (1986) declares English as the official language, and protects the rights of bilinguals in its statutes (2016); the constitution of Louisiana (1974) recognizes "the right of the people to preserve, foster, and promote their respective historic, linguistic and cultural origins"; and the Constitution of New Mexico (1912) establishes provisions to protect the right to vote and hold office regardless of English speaking, reading, or writing ability (Articles 7, 21), access to bilingual education for children of Hispanic descent (Article 12), and the right to receive legal information in Spanish from the government (Article 20).

The United States has never had an official language, and attempts to declare English its official language by constitutional amendment have been unsuccessful in the U.S. Congress (King, 1999). However, as noted above, this has not prevented many states from enacting language legislation in their state constitutions or in statute. Such official-English and English-only legislation has been consistently deemed unconstitutional (i.e., a violation of First, Fifth, Sixth, or Fourteenth Amendment rights) by the supreme courts of several states, federal district courts, and a multitude of legal commentators (see, for example, Crawford, 2000; Faingold, 2016a; Robertson, 2001; Sinsheimer, 2005; Zuckerman, 2010). Even though the U.S. government has never specified English as the official language of the country, the absence of an official language in the U.S. Constitution has not prevented the existence of *implicit* language policies in the United States (e.g., hegemonic institutional practices such as the use of English in government operations, the courts, and the educational system) (McKay & Hornberger, 1996; Shohamy, 2006).

This chapter offers a classification and analysis of the constitutions and legal statutes of the fifty states that compose the United States based on the kinds of language recognition they include. Its purpose is to aid U.S. states seeking to draft language legislation as a part of a revision of their constitutions or legal statutes. The analysis, which captures the essence of language legislation found in the constitutions and legal statutes, is based on the status (i.e., official or not official) of languages spoken in each state, as declared in the state's constitution and legal statutes, and on provisions written into the constitution or legal statutes, or the absence thereof, to protect the language rights of the linguistic majority and minorities living in the state.

As noted earlier, certain constitutions and legislative statutes of U.S. states establish English as official with explicit provisions to protect the language rights of the speakers of the official language (Alabama, Arizona, Arkansas, Colorado, Florida, Georgia, Idaho, Iowa, Kansas, Missouri, Montana, Nebraska New Hampshire, North Carolina, Oklahoma, South Carolina, South Dakota, Tennessee, Utah, Virginia, West Virginia, and Wyoming). The purpose of such provisions is to enable enforcement of the official-English laws (Sinsheimer, 2005). In contrast, other states establish laws that declare the status of English as official without explicit provisions in the legislative statutes to protect the language rights of speakers of the official language (Illinois, Indiana, Kentucky, Mississippi, and North Dakota). Because they lack provisions for legal enforcement, these laws are mostly symbolic (Sinsheimer, 2005). Still other states do not mention any language rights and establish no official language in their constitutions or in statute (Alaska, Connecticut, Delaware, Maine, Maryland, Massachusetts, Michigan, Minnesota, Nevada, New Jersey, New York, Ohio, Oregon, Pennsylvania, Rhode Island, Texas, Vermont, Washington, and Wisconsin). As noted, the states of Louisiana and New Mexico do not mention an official language, but provide provisions to protect the linguistic rights of indigenous minorities in the state (i.e., Spanish and French in Louisiana and Spanish in New Mexico). The Constitution of California declares English as the official language, but protects the rights of bilinguals in its statutes. The constitution of Hawaii establishes the official status of both English and Hawaiian, as well as provisions for its indigenous minority language (i.e., Hawaiian).

CLASSIFICATIONS

In this study, the constitutions and other legal statutes of every U.S. state were screened exhaustively to identify legal language defining the linguistic obligations of the state and the language rights of individuals and groups. The following seven classifications begin with states that do not have explicit language legislation in their constitutions—that is, states that do not declare any official language and have no provisions in their constitution or other statutes defining language obligations or language rights for their residents. Subsequent classifications identify states that do include explicit legal provisions related to language—for example, by defining English as official and/or establishing language provisions that define the linguistic obligations of the state or protect the rights of citizens to use or develop majority and minority languages.

Constitutional Provisions

Type 1: No official language; no provisions. Nineteen states are silent on language in their constitutions. They (1) designate no official language, (2) establish no language provisions granting language rights to individuals and groups, and (3) specify no linguistic obligations toward their citizens. These states are Alaska, Connecticut, Delaware, Maine, Maryland, Massachusetts, Michigan, Minnesota, Nevada, New Jersey, New York, Ohio, Oregon, Pennsylvania, Rhode Island, Texas, Vermont, Washington, and Wisconsin.

Type 2: No official language; provisions for minorities. New Mexico (1912) and Louisiana (1974) (1) designate no official language, and (2) establish provisions for minorities in their constitutions.

Type 3: Official English; provisions for official English. Nebraska (1920), Colorado (1988), Florida (1988), Alabama (1990), Arizona (2006), Missouri (2008), and Oklahoma (2010) (1) designate English as the official language, and (2) establish language provisions to protect the official language.

Type 4: Official English and Hawaiian; provisions for a minority. Hawaii (1978) (1) declares English and Hawaiian as official languages, and (2) establishes provisions for minority speakers of Hawaiian in its constitution.

Type 5: Official English in the constitution; provisions for minorities in its statutes. California (1) declares English as the official language (1986), and (2) protects the rights of bilinguals in its statutes.

Statutory Provisions

Type 6: Official English; no provisions. Illinois (1969), Indiana (1984), Kentucky (1984), Mississippi (1987), and North Dakota (1987) (1) designate English as the official language, but (2) do not establish any provisions to protect the language rights of individuals or groups, and (3) do not specify any linguistic obligations toward their citizens in their statutes.

Type 7: Official English; provisions for official English. Tennessee (1984), Arkansas (1987), North Carolina (1987), South Carolina (1987), Montana (1995), New Hampshire (1995), South Dakota (1995), Georgia (1996), Virginia (1996), Wyoming (1996), Utah (2000), Iowa (2002), Idaho (2007), Kansas (2007), and West Virginia (2016) (1) designate English as the official language, and (2) establish language provisions to protect the official language in their statutes.

ANALYSIS

With these seven classifications, we can distinguish two approaches to the languages spoken in a state: the "hands-on" approach, concerned with codifying language requirements by constitutional amendment or statutory enactment, and the "hands-off" approach, which is not concerned with codifying language requirements and instead assumes that the state should "leave language alone" (Faingold, 2004a, pp. 18–19; King, 1999, pp. 9).

An analysis of language legislation in the constitutions and statutes of the states in the United States reveals (1) two indicators of a hands-off approach: (a) no official language and (b) no language provisions; and five indicators of a hands-on approach: (a) official languages, (b) language provisions for official languages, (c) language provisions for the minority, and (d) language provisions for the majority. In a hands-off approach, a state opts not to promulgate an official language, nor does it draft any provision specifying language rights or obligations by the government or its citizens. In a hands-on approach, the state opts for the promulgation of one or more official languages. It may also opt for drafting language provisions that specify the language rights of official languages and other languages (Faingold, 2004a).

A hands-on/hands-off analysis of the fifty states of the United States reveals that nineteen states (38 percent of the states in the United States) are deemed hands-off because two hands-off indicators apply in the construction of these types of legislation. In contrast, thirty-one states (62 percent of the states in the United States) are regarded as hands-on because one or more hands-on indicators apply in the construction of these types of legislation (Faingold, 2004a). Yet, those thirty-one states adopting "hands-on" indicators fail Faingold's (2004a) litmus test for "divided" states because they are not divided in a geopolitical sense; that is, they do not have unassimilated language groups possessing or seeking autonomy or secession. Thus, regardless of the type of legislation adopted (i.e., hands-off or hands-on), there are no "divided" states in the United States because they all have (or declare that they have) a strong sense of national identity; and further, these states have no groups possessing or seeking autonomy or secession (Faingold, 2004a, p. 19), unlike divided nations such as Belgium, Canada, and Spain (Faingold, 2004a, 2007; Ricento, 1996; Schiffman, 1996; Veltman, 1983, 1988).

Non-nativist and Nativist Language Policies in the United States

An analysis in terms of non-nativist and nativist legal approaches preferred by the states in the United States reveals that 23 states (46 percent of U.S. states) are deemed non-nativist because their legal systems are favorable, or are at least neutral, toward the linguistic practices of both majority and minority groups. Non-nativist states such as those in Type 1 are silent on language in their constitutions and are in tandem with the U.S. Constitution. Similarly, the states of Louisiana and New Mexico (Type 2), the state of Hawaii (Type 4), and the state of California (Type 5) are deemed non-nativist because they declare provisions to protect the rights of language minorities. Massachusetts does not have a statute declaring English as the official language of the state; however, in a 1975 court case—the one and only case of this kind in the history of Massachusetts—the Supreme Court of this state held that a notification to vacate condemned apartments that was printed only in English was sufficient notice to the non-English-speaking tenants such that their failure to vacate could warrant criminal charges. Somewhat mendaciously, the Official English movement website has been claiming for years that this ruling is just the same as if Massachusetts had declared English as the official language of the state, in spite of the fact that Massachusetts has never done so by constitutional amendment or by statute. Similarly, the Official English website claims that English has been the official language of Alaska since 1998, even though in 2002 the Supreme Court of the State of Alaska declared the 1998 law unconstitutional. In addition, Official English claims that English has been the official language of Louisiana since 1812, in spite of the fact that Louisiana has never declared English its official language in its state constitution nor in statute. This is an amazing claim, considering that the State of Louisiana is one of just four states (the other three are California, Hawaii, and New Mexico) declaring provisions to protect the rights of its indigenous minority groups. In contrast, 27 states (54 percent of U.S. states) are deemed nativist because their legal systems are non-neutral and reflect, in Crawford's words (2000, p. 24), "anxieties and animosities, insecurities and prejudices" toward the linguistic practices of minority groups. Nativist states such as those in Type 3 declare English as the official language as well as provisions to protect the official language in the state constitution and are not consistent with the U.S. Constitution, which is silent on language. Similarly, nativist states such as those in Type 6 and Type 7 declare English as the official language in their statutes; states in Type 7, in addition, declare provisions to protect the official language in their statutes. As with Type 3, statutes in Type 6 and Type 7 are also hard to reconcile with the U.S. Constitution, which, as noted, is silent on language (Faingold, 2004a). Types 4 and 5, which declare official languages in the state constitution are hard to reconcile with the U.S. Constitution as well, since neither of the constitutions of these states is silent on language. Nevertheless, as noted, Hawaii and California are deemed non-nativist because they established provisions for speakers of minority languages in the constitution or statutes. Finally, language legislation in nativist states may be inconsistent with the U.S. Constitution and the Civil Rights Act of 1964, which contain legislation protecting speech and the civil rights of all people, including minorities, living in the United States (Faingold, 2006, 2012a, 2016a).

CONCLUSION

The absence of an explicit language policy in hands-off states has not prevented such states (and the nation as a whole) from practicing implicit language policies (e.g., in government operations, such as the courts and the educational system), that promote the use of English while also allowing other widely spoken languages to be maintained in their speech communities. As a result, as Fishman (2006, p. 325) puts it succinctly, "within the borders of the United States . . . not a single immigrant tongue has reached a self-sustaining level (not even Spanish in our days) in over 200 years."

In the United States, language conflict could be minimized by adopting a less nativist, more inclusive, approach to the enacting of language laws in state constitutions and statutes. For example, as in states which do not mention any language rights and establish no official language in their constitutions or in statute (i.e., Alaska, Connecticut, Delaware, Maine, Maryland, Massachusetts, Michigan, Minnesota, Nevada, New Jersey, New York, Ohio, Oregon, Pennsylvania, Rhode Island, Texas, Vermont, Washington, and Wisconsin); or as in the constitutions and statutes of the states of California, Hawaii, Louisiana, and New Mexico which produced language laws that protect the language rights of linguistic minorities in the United States (see chapter 6; see, also, Faingold, 2006, 2012a, 2016a).

TWO

Language Rights in the Territories of the United States and the Freely Associated States

All attempts to declare English as the official language of the United States by constitutional amendment have failed in the U.S. Congress. Yet, the absence of an official language has not prevented establishing implicit language policies in the United States—for example, the almost exclusive use of English in government operations, the courts, and the educational system (McKay & Hornberger, 1996; Shohamy, 2006). In addition, as we have seen in the previous chapter, the lack of an official language in the U.S. Constitution has not prevented many states in the United States from enacting language legislation in their state constitutions or in statute (Faingold, 2012b, 2013, 2016a). For example, the constitutions of the states of Nebraska (1920), California (1986), Colorado (1988), Florida (1988), Alabama (1990), Arizona (2006), Missouri (2008), and Oklahoma (2010) declare English as the official language of the state and establish language provisions that define the linguistic obligations of the state and citizens toward the official language, without enacting protections for minority languages. Similarly, the legal statutes of Tennessee (1984), Arkansas, North Carolina and South Carolina (1987), Montana, New Hampshire and South Dakota (1995), Georgia, Virginia and Wyoming (1996), Utah (2000), Iowa (2002), Idaho and Kansas (2007), and West Virginia (2016) declare English as the official language of the state and declare the linguistic duties of the state and citizens toward the official language, without establishing protections for minority languages. Other states do not mention any language rights and state no official language in their constitutions or in statute (i.e., Alaska, Connecticut, Delaware, Maine, Maryland, Massachusetts, Michigan, Minnesota, Nevada, New Jersey, New

York, Ohio, Oregon, Pennsylvania, Rhode Island, Texas, Vermont, Washington, and Wisconsin). In contrast, the constitution of Hawaii (1978) declares both English and Hawaiian as official languages of Hawaii. The constitutions of Louisiana (1974) and New Mexico (1912) do not mention any official languages, but they enact provisions to protect the language rights of minorities living in the state: Spanish and French in Louisiana and Spanish in New Mexico (see chapter 1; see also, Faingold, 2012b, 2013).

This chapter offers a classification and analysis of the constitutions, organic acts, and statutes of territories of the United States (hence territories) (i.e., Puerto Rico, the United States Virgin Islands, Guam, the Northern Mariana Islands, and American Samoa) and the Freely Associated States (hence associated states) (i.e., the Federated States of Micronesia, the Republic of the Marshall Islands, and the Republic of Palau), based on the kinds of language recognition they include. Its purpose is to aid the United States, including its territories and associated states, to draft language legislation. The analysis, which captures the essence of language legislation found in the constitutions, organic acts, and statutes of these territories and associated states, is based on the status (i.e., official or not official) of languages spoken in the territory or associated state, as declared in their constitutions, organic acts, statutes, and legal provisions written there to protect the language rights of the citizens living in the territory or associated state.

TERRITORIES AND ASSOCIATED STATES

Territories

Since its foundation in 1776, the United States has had areas outside of the original thirteen states which were legally part of the country but were not considered states according to the Territorial Clause of the U.S. Constitution as set in Article 4, Section 3:

> New States may be admitted by the Congress into the Union; but no new State shall be formed or erected within the Jurisdiction of any other State; nor any State be formed by the Junction of two or more States, or Parts of States, without the Consent of the Legislatures of the States concerned as well as of the Congress.

> The Congress shall have the Power to dispose of and make all needful Rules and Regulations respecting the Territory or other Property belonging to the United States; and nothing in this Constitution shall be so construed as to Prejudice any Claims of the United States, or of any particular State. (U.S. Constitution, Article 4, Section 3)

For example, the states of Ohio, Indiana, Illinois, Michigan, Wisconsin, and part of Minnesota were carved out of the Northwest Territory created by Congress in 1787 in the areas west of Pennsylvania, north of the Ohio river, east of the Missouri river, and south of the Great Lakes; the states of Arkansas, Iowa, Kansas, Missouri, Nebraska, Oklahoma, and parts of Minnesota, the Dakotas, Montana, Wyoming, Colorado, and Louisiana from areas west of the Mississippi River, purchased from France in 1803; the states of Arizona, California, Nevada, New Mexico, Utah, and parts of the states of Colorado, Kansas, Wyoming, and Oklahoma from the annexation of the American Southwest in the aftermath of the Mexican American War (1846–1848) and the Treaty of Guadalupe Hidalgo (1848) (Faingold, 2014). In the twentieth century, the territories of Oklahoma (1907), New Mexico and Arizona (1912), and Hawaii and Alaska (1959) became states.

The territories of Puerto Rico (18.24914° N, 66.62804° W) and Guam (13.42113° N, 144.7397° E) were ceded by Spain to the United States in the aftermath of the Spanish American War and the Treaty of Paris (1898) (Grabowski & Grabowski, 1992). The United States Virgin Islands (17.75262° N, 64.73542° W) were purchased from Denmark in 1916, and they became a territory of the United States in 1917 (Dookhan, 1994; Grabowski & Grabowski, 1992). The Northern Mariana Islands (15.26278° N, 145.8046° E) became a territory of the United States in 1976, in the aftermath of the dissolution of the U.S. administration of the United Nations Trust Territory of the Pacific Islands (1947–1986) (Willens & Siemer, 2002). In 1900 the Tui Manu'a, holder of the oldest chiefly title of the Samoa islands, and the other chiefs of Samoa, ceded the islands of Tutuila and Manu'a, Eastern Samoa (14.3° N, 170.7° E), to the United States; they became a territory of the United States in 1951, American Samoa (Grabowski & Grabowski, 1992; Shaffer, 2000).

Territories of the United States are classified according to two major criteria: (a) incorporated or unincorporated, and (b) organized or unorganized.

Incorporated territories are part of the United States (i.e., the U.S. Constitution is in full effect). For example, before they were states, Oklahoma, New Mexico, Arizona, Alaska, and Hawaii were incorporated territories. All other territories are unincorporated territories. Unincorporated territories belong to the United States but are not part of it (i.e., the U.S. Constitution applies only partially) (Leibowitz, 1989).

Organized territories are subject to an Organic Act passed by the U.S. Congress (i.e., the United States Virgin Islands and Guam). Also, territories can have a constitution, if it is passed with congressional consent (i.e., Puerto Rico and the Northern Mariana Islands)—and are often referred to as "Commonwealth." Residents of organized territories are citizens of the United States and are allowed to move to the mainland, but they cannot vote in federal elections. Each organized territory has a representative in the U.S. Congress, which cannot vote on the floor but may vote in committee (Dookhan, 1994; Grabowski & Grabowski, 1992; Leibowitz, 1989; Willens & Siemer, 2002).

There is only one unorganized territory, American Samoa, which has its own constitution (the U.S. Constitution is not in effect in American Samoa) and an elected non-voting delegate in the U.S. Congress. Citizens of American Samoa are U.S. nationals but not citizens of the United States. They can live and work anywhere in the United States, but they cannot vote in federal elections, not even after they move to the U.S. mainland (unless they become citizens of the United States). They are allowed to travel to and settle in the United States without restrictions and can apply for citizenship as if they were resident aliens (Grabowski & Grabowski, 1992; Leibowitz, 1989; Shaffer, 2000).

Associated States

In 1947 the United Nations created a strategic-area trusteeship from former Japanese possessions, the Trust Territory of the Pacific Islands, of which the United States assumed control from 1947 to 1986, until the constituent islands achieved independence (i.e., the Federated States of Micronesia, the Republic of the Marshall Islands, and the Republic of Palau) or became a territory of the United States (i.e., the Northern Mariana Islands) (Grabowski & Grabowski, 1992; Leibowitz, 1989; Willens & Siemer, 2002).

In 1979 both the Republic of the Marshall Islands (7.286208° N, 168.7514° E) and the Federated States of Micronesia (6.869349° N, 158.1873° E) declared independence, followed by the Republic of Palau (7.35° N, 134.4667° E) in 1981 (Leibowitz, 1989). In 1986 the Republic of the Marshall Islands and the Federated States of Micronesia signed a Compact of Free Association with the United States, followed by the Republic of Palau in 1994.

The associated states (i.e., the Federated States of Micronesia, the Republic of the Marshall Islands, and the Republic of Palau) are independent and sovereign nations. However, under the terms of the Compact of Free Association, the United States has full authority and responsibility for the security and defense of the associated states. Their citizens are neither citizens nor nationals of the United States, but they are allowed to work and study in the United States without a visa. The United States provides millions of dollars in economic assistance to the Republic of the Marshall Islands, the Federated States of Micronesia, and the Republic of Palau every year, along with a variety of federal grants and services (Leibowitz, 1989).

CLASSIFICATIONS

The constitutions, organic acts, and statutes of every territory and associated state were screened exhaustively to identify legal language defining the linguistic obligations of the state, and the language rights of individuals and groups. The following classifications identify territories and associated states that include explicit legal provisions related to language—for example, by defining English and another language or languages as official and/or establishing language provisions that define the linguistic obligations of the state, or protect the rights of citizens to use or develop majority and minority languages (i.e., Puerto Rico, Guam, the Northern Mariana Islands, American Samoa, the Republic of the Marshall Islands, the Federated States of Micronesia, and the Republic of Palau). Also, the classifications identify one territory that does not declare any official language and has no language provisions in its organic act or statutes—that is, a territory that does not define language obligations or language rights for its residents (i.e., the United States Virgin Islands).

Organic Provisions in an Unincorporated and Organized Territory

Type 1: No official language; no provisions. The territory of the United States Virgin Islands (1) designates no official language, and (2) establishes no language provisions granting language rights to individuals and groups, and (3) specifies no language obligations toward its citizens in its organic act (1954).

Statutory Provisions in an Unincorporated and Organized Territory

Type 2: Official languages; provisions for official languages. The Commonwealth of Puerto Rico (1) declares English and Spanish as the official languages, and (2) establishes provisions for official English and Spanish in its statutes (2013).

Constitutional and Statutory Provisions in an Unincorporated and Organized Territory

Type 3: Official languages; provisions for official languages; provisions for minority languages. The Commonwealth of the Northern Mariana Islands (1) declares Chamorro, Carolinian, and English as the official languages in its constitution (1978), (2) establishes provisions for official languages in its constitution (1978), and (3) establishes provisions for minority speakers of Chamorro and Carolinian in its statutes (1982, 2007, 2011).

Organic and Statutory Provisions in an Unincorporated and Organized Territory

Type 4: Official languages; provisions for official languages; provisions for minority languages; provisions for all people. The territory of Guam (1) declares English and Chamorro as the official languages in its statutes (1974), (2) establishes provisions for official English in its statutes (1980), (3) establishes provisions for minority speakers of Chamorro in its statutes (1964, 1973, 1977, 1979, 1984, 1991, 1992, 1997, 2002, 2011), and (4) establishes provisions for all people in its organic act (2004).

Constitutional and Statutory Provisions in an Unincorporated and Unorganized Territory

Type 5: No official language; provisions for minority languages. The territory of American Samoa (1) designates no official language, and (2) establishes language provisions for minority speakers of Samoan in its constitution (1967) and in its statutes (2004).

Constitutional Provisions in Associated States

Type 6: No official language; provisions for all people. The Federated States of Micronesia (1978) and the Republic of the Marshall Islands (1979) (1) designate no official language, and (2) establish provisions for all people in their constitutions.

Type 7: Official languages; national languages; provisions for official languages; provisions for all people. The Republic of Palau (1) declares Palau and English as the official languages, (2) declares the Palauan languages as national languages, (3) establishes provisions for official Palau and English, and (4) establishes provisions for all people in its constitution (1980).

ANALYSIS

With these seven classifications we can distinguish two approaches to the languages spoken in a territory or associated state: the "hands-on" approach, concerned with codifying language requirements in the constitution, organic act, or statutes, and the "hands-off" approach, which is not concerned with codifying language requirements (Faingold, 2004a, 2012a, 2012b, 2013). Thus, an analysis of language legislation in the constitutions, organic acts, and statutes of territories and associated states reveals (1) two indicators of a hands-off approach: (a) no official language, and (b) no language provisions; and (2) five indicators of a hands-on approach: (a) official languages, (b) national languages, (c) language provisions for official languages, (d) language provisions for minority languages, and (e) language provisions for all people.

In a hands-off approach, a territory or associated state opts not to promulgate an official language, nor does it draft any provision specifying language rights or obligations by the government or its citizens. In a hands-on approach, the territory or associated state may opt for the promulgation of one or more official languages. It may also opt for drafting language provisions that specify the language rights of official languages and other languages (Faingold, 2004a, 2012a, 2013).

Only one territory (12.5 percent of the territories and associated states) is deemed hands-off (i.e., the United States Virgin Islands) because two hands-off indicators apply in the construction of this type of legislation. In contrast, seven territories and associated states (87.5 percent of the territories and associated states) are regarded as hands-on (i.e., Puerto Rico, Guam, the Northern Mariana Islands, American Samoa, the Republic of the Marshall Islands, the Federated States of Micronesia, and the Republic of Palau) because one or more hands-on indicators apply in the construction of these types of legislation (Faingold, 2004a, 2012b, 2013).

CONCLUSION

Unlike many states in the United States which declare English as the sole official language and/or enact provisions to protect official English (i.e., Alabama, Arizona, Arkansas, Colorado, Florida, Georgia, Idaho, Iowa, Kansas, Missouri, Montana, Nebraska, New Hampshire, North Carolina, Oklahoma, South Carolina, South Dakota, Tennessee, Utah, Virginia, West Virginia, and Wyoming) (Faingold, 2012b, 2013), none of the territories and associated states declares English as the sole official language or establishes provisions that hinder the rights of language minority groups of the territory or associated state.

Under the United States Virgin Islands' Organic Act of 1936, the vote was limited to voters who could read and write the English language (Dookhan, 1994; Leibowitz, 1989). The Revised Organic Act of 1954 "abolished the language qualification for voters" (Dookhan, 1994, p. 291). As noted by Leibowitz (1989), "in order not to exclude immigrants from Puerto Rico from the franchise, the English literacy requirement was dropped, and the legislature was prohibited from establishing any literacy requirement" (p. 255). However, as in many other states in the United States (i.e., Alaska, Connecticut, Delaware, Maine, Maryland, Massachusetts, Michigan, Minnesota, Nevada, New Jersey, New York, Ohio, Oregon, Pennsylvania, Rhode Island, Texas, Vermont, Washington, and Wisconsin (Faingold, 2012b, 2013), the absence of an explicit language policy in the United States Virgin Islands' Revised Organic Act of 1954 has not prevented it from practicing implicit language policies (e.g., in government operations, such as the courts and the educational system) that promote the use of English while also allowing minority languages to be used in the community (Leibowitz, 1989). For example, "schools in St. Croix now (1989) feature a bilingual program serving 3,000 (Puerto Rican) students" (Leibowitz, 1989, p. 228).

As in a few states in the United States (i.e., California, Hawaii, Louisiana, and New Mexico) (Faingold, 2012b, 2013), with the exception of the United States Virgin Islands (see above), all other territories and associated states have established hands-on policies declaring provisions that protect the rights of language minority groups, or of all people living in the territory or associated state. For example, in Guam, Public Law 14–53, Section 11682 (1977) declares:

> Chamorro language and culture courses mandatory. The Department shall include courses in Chamorro language and culture in its curriculum. Such courses shall be mandatory upon the development of a complete Chamorro Language and Culture Program but not later than the school year 1980 for all elementary students but elective for students in the junior and senior high schools. (Public Law 14–53, Section 11682)

Similarly, Section 3 of the Constitution of American Samoa declares that:

> It shall be the policy of the Government of American Samoa to protect persons of Samoan ancestry against alienation of their lands and the destruction of the Samoan way of life and language, contrary to their best interests. Such legislation as may be necessary may be enacted to protect the lands, customs, culture, and traditional Samoan family organization of persons of Samoan ancestry. (Constitution of American Samoa, 1967)

An additional example would be Article 22, Section 3 of the Northern Mariana Islands' Constitution:

> The official language of the Commonwealth shall be Chamorro, Carolinian and English, as deemed appropriate and as enforced by the legislature. The legislature may provide that government proceedings and documents shall be in at least one of the three languages. This section shall not be subject to judicial review. (Northern Mariana Islands Constitution, 1978)

Similarly, Title 1, Chapter 5, Section 59 (2013) of the legal statutes of Puerto Rico states that:

> Spanish and English are established as official languages of the Government of Puerto Rico. Both languages may be used, indistinctively, in all departments, municipalities or other political subdivisions, agencies, public corporations, offices and government dependencies of the Executive, Legislative and Judiciary Branches of the Commonwealth of Puerto Rico, pursuant to the provisions of §§ 59--59f of this title, or by that which is provided by a special law. (Laws of Puerto Rico, Title 1, Chapter 5, Section 59).

Finally, under the nativist English-only ideology now regnant in most of the states in the United States (Faingold, 2012b, 2016a), it seems doubtful that the Commonwealth of Puerto Rico, where the majority of the population favors statehood, will be allowed to join the United States without the abandonment of its indigenous official language (i.e., Spanish) (Barreto, 2001).

Fifty years ago, U.S. Senator Henry Jackson already underlined the language issue in Puerto Rico in relation to statehood from a nativist English-only perspective:

> The unity of our Federal State structure . . . requires a common tongue. We do not have to look far to see what has happened in certain countries that have failed to adhere to this fundamental practice. Surely, at a time when we are trying to eliminate ghettos of all kinds (1966), we should not establish within our Federal-State system a "language ghetto." A condition precedent to Statehood must be the recognition of English as the official language. (Status Commission Report, 1966, p. 22; cited by Leibowitz, 1989, p. 153)

II

U.S. Federal Language Rights Legislation

THREE

Language Rights in the U.S. Constitution and the Civil Rights Act of 1964

The present chapter analyzes the Fourteenth Amendment of the U.S. Constitution and the Civil Rights Act of 1964 for language that defines the linguistic obligations of the United States and the language rights of persons in the United States, arguing that neither the U.S. Constitution nor the Civil Rights Act of 1964 define de jure obligations of the United States toward members of language minorities. It argues that the United States should explicitly recognize the language rights of minority groups in the United States. In addition, the chapter aims to provide expert advice about language policy to aid political decision-makers of the United States in interpreting existing legislation and drafting new legislation to help solve linguistic conflicts arising among speakers of majority and minority languages (Faingold, 2004a, 2007, 2012b, 2016a). Future interpretations of existing laws and statutes and new legislation addressing the rights of speakers of minority languages to equal protection status under the Fourteenth Amendment and the Civil Rights Act of 1964 are more likely to help solve conflicts by defining legally the status of speakers of such languages.

Since its formation more than two hundred years ago, the United States has been a multilingual country. Ricento (1996) notes that its multilingual character has remained constant since pre-colonial times due to uninterrupted immigration. When large numbers of immigrants settled in areas of low population density, they were frequently able to use their languages for public purposes, including education (e.g., German-speakers in rural Illinois, Minnesota, Ohio, Pennsylvania, and Wisconsin as well as Spanish-speakers in California and the Southwest). Further, Del

Valle (2003) notes that, during the first years of the republic, bilingualism and multilingualism were not only much more prevalent than today amongst the population as a whole, but the use of minority languages was officially sanctioned by the state and local governments. The fostering of minority languages helped the government to bring together different peoples around the founding political principles of the United States: democracy, republicanism, and constitutionalism, and showing that the government bore no ill will toward language-minority communities.

However, over the years, the use of languages other than English in the public arena, especially in education, has become less tolerated. Over the past two hundred and fifty years, according to Ricento (1996, p. 152), the United States became less tolerant toward indigenous and immigrant groups, mostly non-white and non-European, showed a tendency toward cultural isolationism and monolingualism, and expressed the belief that immigrants should abandon their culture and stop using their native languages in order to become "American."

THE FOURTEENTH AMENDMENT OF THE U.S. CONSTITUTION AND THE CIVIL RIGHTS ACT OF 1964

The following sections identify passages in the Fourteenth Amendment of the U.S. Constitution and the Civil Rights Act of 1964 that appear to recognize *de facto* linguistic rights of language minorities in the United States. I will deal with each of these in turn.

The Fourteenth Amendment, Section 1

Enacted during reconstruction and three years after the Thirteenth Amendment, the Fourteenth Amendment attempted to put the newly freed slaves on an equal footing with White men and to protect them from those who would seek to undermine the spirit, if not the letter, of the Thirteenth Amendment which prohibited slavery in the United States. To this end, the Fourteenth Amendment, Section 1, of the U.S. Constitution establishes that "No State shall . . . deprive any person of life, liberty, or property, without due process of law; nor deny to any person within its jurisdiction the equal protection of the laws (U.S. Constitution, Fourteenth Amendment, Section 1)."

The Fourteenth Amendment contains these two clauses that language minorities have traditionally looked for to bring claims of linguistic discrimination under the law: The Due Process and the Equal Protection Clauses. The latter is of especial importance because it prohibits racial and ethnic discrimination. The Due Process Clause guarantees a fair procedure. The individual to be dispossessed of a right must be afforded notice of that possibility and an opportunity to be heard. Thus, the method (i.e., the language) chosen to give notice must be reasonably calculated to inform interested parties of the pendency of the action and afford them an opportunity to present their objections. The Equal Protection Clause prohibits racial and ethnic discrimination, guarantees an evenhanded administration of the laws (i.e., equal treatment by courts and law enforcement agencies) and prohibits discrimination on the basis of an individual's race, ancestry, national origin, or ethnicity (Del Valle, 2003). Further, as Del Valle notes, "reading the Fourteenth Amendment broadly to cover substantive as well as procedural rights and to protect ethnic as well as racial minorities (is) absolutely essential if the Civil Rights Amendments (are) to have life into the twentieth and twenty-first centuries (pp. 45–46)."

The Civil Rights Act of 1964

The Civil Rights Act of 1964 was enacted by the Senate and House of Representatives—the 88th Congress—of the United States of America. Titles VI and VII protect minorities from discrimination by the majority in federally assisted programs and in the workplace respectively, because of their race, color, religion, sex, or national origin. As it is stated in the preamble, the aim of the Act is:

> To enforce the constitutional right to vote, to confer jurisdiction upon the district courts of the United States to provide injunctive relief against discrimination in public accommodations, to authorize the Attorney General to institute suits to protect constitutional rights in public facilities and public education, to extend the Commission of Civil Rights, to prevent discrimination in federally assisted programs, to establish a Commission of Equal Employment Opportunity, and for other purposes. (Civil Rights Act of 1964, Preamble)

Title VI—Nondiscrimination in Federally Assisted Programs

Title VI of the Civil Rights Act of 1964 states that "No person in the United States shall, on the grounds of race, color, or national origin, be excluded from participation in, be denied the benefits of, or be subjected to discrimination under any program or activity receiving Federal financial assistance (Civil Rights Act of 1964, Title VI)." It prohibits any program receiving Federal financial assistance from discrimination. To enforce this statute the Office of Civil Rights was created. This office relies mostly on reconciliation between parties and almost never litigates cases. Title VI has been used to combat English-only rules in states that passed amendments making English the official language of the state. For example, in 1990 the state of Alabama passed a constitutional amendment to make English the official language of the state (Amendment 509)—a so-called English-only law. The purpose of such laws is to eradicate all non-English languages from every state or local government office and document, and especially to prohibit employees from speaking a foreign language on the job. Amendment 509 states:

> English is the official language of the state of Alabama. The legislature shall enforce this amendment by appropriate legislation. The legislature and officials of the state of Alabama shall take all steps necessary to insure that the role of English as the common language of the state of Alabama is preserved and enhanced. The legislature shall make no law which diminishes or ignores the role of English as the common language of the state of Alabama. (Alabama Constitution, 2010)

About one year after Amendment 509 passed, the Department of Public Safety of the state of Alabama adopted an English-only policy requiring all portions of the driver's license test, including the written exam, to be given in English only. The use of interpreters, translation, dictionaries, and so forth, was officially prohibited. Before the passage of the Amendment, Alabama, like most other states, had conducted the written portion of its driver's license exam in many foreign languages. Martha Sandoval, a driver's license applicant who lacked proficiency in English, brought a class action suit in district court on her behalf and that of others under Title VI of the Civil Rights Act. Title VI prohibits governmental agencies from implementing policies or practices that have a discriminatory impact, even if they were not implemented or created with intent to actually discriminate. However, only race, ethnicity, and national origin are specified as illegal bases for discrimination under the Act. The defendants argued that the English-only policy discriminates on the basis of language, not national origin, and that language is not equivalent to national origin. The court's common sense analysis, however, disagreed, finding in favor of the plaintiffs, noting the strong ties between language and national origin often found by federal courts and government agencies, and concluding that an English-only policy could indeed violate Title VI on the basis of national origin. The district's court decision was appealed to the Eleventh Circuit on the grounds of whether there is a right of action for private citizens under Title VI. In 1999, the district court decided that indeed there was right of action because of the discriminatory nature of English-only policies as well as the weakly constructed bureaucratic arguments made by the defendants. The circuit court's decision was appealed to the Supreme Court where the earlier decision was reversed on the technical question of whether private citizens can sue under the statute. The Supreme Court decided that individuals cannot sue under Title VI, undermining the viability of discrimination claims under the statute (Del Valle, 2003).

Title VII—Discrimination Because of Race, Color, Religion, Sex, or National Origin

Title VII of the Civil Rights Act of 1964 states that

> It shall be an unlawful employment practice to an employer—
>
> 1. to fail or refuse to hire or to discharge any individual, or otherwise discriminate against any individual with respect to his compensation, terms, conditions, or privileges of employment, because of such individual's race, color, religion, sex, or national origin; or
> 2. to limit, segregate, or classify his employees in any way which would deprive or tend to deprive any individual of employment opportunities or otherwise adversely affect his status as an employee, because of such individual's race, color, religion, sex, or national origin. (Civil Rights Act of 1964, Title VII)

Title VII of the Civil Rights Act of 1964 prohibits employer discrimination. It applies to private employers as well as state and local government employers, labor organizations, and employment agencies. Title VII has been used to combat English-only rules in the workplace. Many employees possess the ability to use a foreign language, especially Spanish, and sometimes use it along with English in the workplace. In some cases, employers have made rules against speaking all foreign languages—English-only policies—in the workplace (Faingold, 2006, 2012b, 2016a). In a number of cases, with the aid of the Equal Employment Opportunity Commission (EEOC), the administrative agency created to enforce the statute, English-only policies have been challenged by bilingual employees in U.S. courts. As Del Valle (2003, pp. 120–121) notes

> The EEOC (brings) employers to court, and wins financial judgments against them. . . . In 1980, the EEOC adopted Guidelines on Discrimination Because of National Origin, which defines national-origin discrimination broadly as including, but not limited to, "the denial of equal employment opportunity because of an individual's or his or her ancestor's place of origin; or because an individual has the physical, cultural or *linguistic* (emphasis added) characteristics of a national origin group. . . . The EEOC has explained that it believes "an individual primary language is often an essential national origin characteristic" and that a rule requiring employees to speak only English at all times in the workplace is a burdensome term and condition of employment

> that violates Title VII except in limited circumstances. (Del Valle, 2003, pp. 120–121)

According to the EEOC Guidelines, employer rules and requirements to speak only English in the workplace can create an atmosphere of inferiority, intimidation, and xenophobia. According to the EEOC, moreover, the employer needs to show a legitimate and clearly articulated business necessity for such rules and requirements (Del Valle, 2003; Krahnke et al., 2003). Krahnke et al. (2003) present examples of recent cases that were decided in accordance with EEOC guidelines:

> In 1999, in Martinez v. Lenox Health Care and Vencor, Inc., a US District Court in California ruled against an employer who established English-only regulations in a nursing home work setting. Employees were disciplined for speaking a non-English language among themselves, contrary to rules established by the employer. . . . In 2000, the Federal Court of the Northern District of Illinois, Eastern Division settled a suit that eight former employees had brought against Watlow Batavia, Inc. for disciplining the workers for speaking Spanish with co-workers on an assembly line. . . . In April, 2001, the EEOC reached a landmark settlement against the University of Incarnate Word (UIW). . . in San Antonio, Texas, for 18 Hispanic housekeepers who were forbidden to use their Spanish native language. (Krahnke et al., 2003)

More recently, in 2006, in *Maldonado v. City of Altus*, the Tenth Circuit U.S. Court of Appeals (covering Colorado, Kansas, Oklahoma, New Mexico, Utah, and Wyoming) ruled that an employer's English-only policy prohibiting employees from speaking any language except English at work could violate Federal anti-discrimination statutes. The case involved claims by 29 Hispanic public employees of the City of Altus, Oklahoma. The policy was created by the City after complaints by English-speaking employers and employees that they could not understand what was being said on the City radio by Spanish-speaking employees. However, the policy, which was initially created to deal with this specific problem, soon became much broader in both its terms and applications. The policy stated that "all work related and business communications during the workday shall be conducted in the English language with the exception of those circumstances where it is necessary or prudent to communicate with a citizen, business owner, organization or criminal suspect in his or her native language due to the person's or entity's limited English language skills" (Administrative Policy # 1.13, 2002, p.1). The policy covered all forms of written and oral communication between co-workers, at all times except private communications during lunch-time, breaks, and conversations with family members. However, the policy was applied to Spanish-speaking employees immediately to prohibit private oral communications during lunch-time and breaks and even during telephone conversations with family members. Because of the policy, the Spanish-speaking employees were continuously taunted and mocked by Anglo employees. The policy created a hostile work environment (Faingold, 2006, 2011, 2016a).

The EEOC determined that the City had committed a violation of Title VII on the basis that the policy was overly broad and discriminatory. English-only workplace rules that *apply at all times* are a burdensome term and condition of employment and a presumed violation of Title VII. Moreover, the EEOC guidelines also state that even in cases when English-only rules *do not apply at all times*, the employer still must justify a business necessity for the rule (Fisher & Phillips, 2006). Although other courts, including the federal district court of Oklahoma in *Maldonado*, had previously rejected EEOC guidelines regarding English-only under Titles VI and VII of the Civil Rights Act of 1964, the Tenth Circuit Court reversed the lower court with regard to the City of Altus Spanish-speaking employees' claims of discrimination under Title VII. Thus, the Circuit Court decided that there was no evidence of a valid business reason for the policy. In addition, the Spanish-speaking employees produced evidence that the policy covered lunch and other breaks as well as private phone conversations. By the end of the court proceedings, the City had conceded that there was no business reason for such restrictions. The Court ruled that the plaintiffs produced sufficient evidence that the City intended the policy to discriminate against Spanish-speaking employees and that the City realized that the policy would lead to taunting by English-speaking personnel (Crapo, 2006; Faingold, 2006, 2016a). The Court held that the fact that the City would forbid Hispanics from using their preferred language could reasonably be construed as an expression of hostility toward Hispanics. The Court noted that there could be unlawful hostility if an employer required an employee calling home during a work break to speak only English. Most importantly, the Circuit Court upheld the presumptions put forward by the EEOC when it noted that "for (the Court) purposes, it is enough that the EEOC, based on its expertise and experience, has consistently concluded that an English-only policy, at least when no business need for the policy is shown, is likely to create an atmosphere of inferiority, isolation and intimidation that constitutes a discriminatory work environment" (http://www.klehr.com/Articles/labor_summer06.html).

However, in a previous case titled *Garcia v. Spun Steak* (1980), the U.S. Court of Appeals for the Ninth Circuit (covering California, Oregon, Washington, Arizona, Montana, Idaho, Nevada, Alaska, Hawaii, Guam, and Northern Marianas) rejected the EEOC guidelines that English-only rules which apply at all times are a burdensome term and condition of employment and a presumed violation of Title VII. In 1990, employees Garcia and Butrago sued Spun Steak in the U.S. District Court of the Northern District of California after the meat company inflicted an English-only rule on its thirty employees. The employees alleged that the English-only policy violated Title VII. The district court ruled that English-only rules violate federal anti-bias rules, but the Ninth Court of Appeals reversed the district court, holding that, in this case, most of the employees were bilingual, so, the court argued, Spun Steak did not violate their rights when it required them to speak English at work. The case went all the way to the U.S. Supreme Court. In 1994 the Supreme Court let stand the Ninth Circuit Court ruling that English-only rules in the workplace do not discriminate against Spanish-speaking employees (http://migration.ucdavis.edu/mn/more.php?id=444_0_2_0). Similarly, in *Dimaranan v. Pomona Valley Hospital* (1991), District Court in California ruled that a "No Tagalog" rule did not violate Title VII because in this case the rule applied to the evening shift of a unit and only to those employees speaking Tagalog.

Thus, as we can see, language rights cases in the United States can yield contradictory results. Judges have a lot of leeway in deciding whether the linguistic rights of minority language speakers have been violated. Judges are quite free to impose their own values and often apply common sense rather than a close reading of the law. In short, mixed outcomes of litigation reflect the lack of a clear de jure definition of language as a protected class. In language rights cases the law seems to lack transparency and determinacy.

LEGISLATING LANGUAGE RIGHTS OF MINORITY LANGUAGES IN THE UNITED STATES

In the sections above I have identified a problem of transparency and determinacy in linguistic law. Outcomes of litigation in the areas of language rights have been mixed, in my opinion, because the Fourteenth Amendment and the Civil Rights Act of 1964 do not define the right of language minorities de jure. For this reason, the United States needs to define the linguistic rights of minority languages de jure (e.g., by constitutional amendment or by enacting new civil rights legislation in its statutes) (Faingold, 2012b). For example, the Constitution of the State of Louisiana states that "the right of the people to preserve, foster, and promote their respective historic, linguistic, and cultural origins is recognized" (Louisiana Constitution, 2010). In addition, or instead, the U.S. Congress can define the term national origin to cover language de jure in future civil rights acts (e.g., by amending the Civil Rights Act of 1964, adding language to the protected categories "race, color, religion, sex, or national origin"). To be sure, the Civil Rights Act of 1964, a key piece of legislation, explicitly targets national, along with racial, sexual and religious, minorities for protection against discrimination but fails to target language minorities for protection. It is unclear as to what languages and linguistic practices are covered under the notion of "national origin."

CONCLUSION

I have analyzed the Fourteenth Amendment of the U.S. Constitution and the Civil Rights Act of 1964 for language that defines the linguistic obligations of the United States and the language rights of persons in the United States. I have shown that neither the U.S. Constitution nor the Civil Rights Act of 1964 defines de jure obligations of the United States toward members of language minorities. I argued that the United States should consider granting certain language rights to minority groups by drafting new legislation to help solve linguistic conflicts arising among speakers of majority and minority languages in this country. This is because U.S. law is unclear as to what linguistic rights and practices are covered by the term "national origin" as a protected group in the Civil Rights Act of 1964, and as a result, outcomes of litigation in U.S. courts have been generally mixed and opaque. Future interpretations of existing laws and statutes, and new legislation addressing the rights of speakers of minority languages to Equal Protection status under the U.S. Constitution and the Civil Rights Act of 1964, are more likely to help solve conflicts by defining legally the status of speakers of such languages.

FOUR

Language Rights in the Workplace in the United States

Code-switching, or moving between one language and another in conversation (Myers-Scotton, 1990; Poplack, 2000), is often considered an inappropriate behavior by teachers and school officials who spend a lot of energy fighting it in the classroom and in other school settings (Palmer, 2009). Similarly, some employers make rules that prohibit code-switching and speaking foreign languages in general at work. This chapter reviews relevant neurocognitive, psycholinguistic, and sociolinguistic literature dealing with code-switching in a variety of settings. It attempts to provide a better understanding of linguistic evidence that can be used to establish a legal framework for the protection of linguistic minorities (Faingold, 2004a, 2006, 2007, 2012a, 2012b, 2014, 2015, 2016b). The chapter focuses on the use of Spanish/English code-switching by Hispanics in the workplace and studies rules that employers make to prohibit this behavior. It argues that code-switching is often not a matter of choice but a natural behavior that occurs unconsciously and unintentionally among bilinguals. Also, the chapter argues that code-switching is crucially connected to the national origin of the speakers and is of social and cultural importance to Hispanics in the United States (Haugen, 1956; Lipski, 1985; Zentella, 1997). The prohibition against speaking foreign languages at work—English-only policies—has been declared illegal under the Civil Rights Act of 1964 by some U.S. courts (Del Valle, 2003; Faingold, 2006, 2012b; Krahnke et al., 2003). The chapter is based on an expert witness report written by the author for the plaintiffs in a language discrimination case in Oklahoma (*Maldonado v. City of Altus,* 2006). The case was settled in favor of the plaintiffs in 2006 (City of Altus Council Meeting Minutes, October 3, 2006). The judgment in this case may constitute a landmark decision establishing a precedent that could affect the outcome of future English-only cases pursued following the EEOC Guidelines. The reason is that the decision "may create a split in the circuit courts" because "a genuine issue of material fact existed as to the presence of a hostile work environment based solely on the employer's adoption of an English-only policy in the workplace" (Thomas, 2007, p. 2).

ENGLISH-ONLY IN THE WORKPLACE

Title VII of the Civil Rights Act of 1964 is the legal instrument used by the Equal Employment Opportunity Commission (EEOC), the administrative agency created to enforce the statute, to combat English-only rules in the workplace in the United States. Many employees possess the ability to use a foreign language and sometimes use it along with English in the workplace. In some cases, employers make rules prohibiting employees from speaking foreign languages and have enacted English-only policies in the workplace (Del Valle, 2003).

Title VII—Discrimination Because of Race, Color, Religion, Sex, or National Origin

> . . . It shall be an unlawful employment practice for an employer—
>
> 1. to fail or refuse to hire or to discharge any individual, or otherwise discriminate against any individual with respect to his compensation, terms, conditions, or privileges of employment, because of such individual's race, color, religion, sex, or national origin; or
> 2. to limit, segregate, or classify his employees in any way which would deprive or tend to deprive any individual of employment opportunities or otherwise adversely affect his status as an employee, because of such individual's race, color, religion, sex, or national origin. (Civil Rights Act of 1964, Title VII)

In a number of cases, English-only policies in the workplace have been challenged by the EEOC in U.S. courts. In 1980 the EEOC created a number of guidelines to be applied in cases of discrimination in which national origin is at issue. The guidelines define national origin discrimination broadly to include linguistic characteristics of a national origin group and specifically address English-only rules, written or unwritten, that prohibit the speaking of languages other than English in the workplace. An individual's primary language is deemed to be an essential national origin characteristic. A rule requiring employees to speak only English at all times in the workplace can be considered a burdensome term and condition of employment that violates Title VII (Del Valle, 2003). Employer rules and requirements to speak only English in the workplace can create an atmosphere of inferiority, intimidation, and xenophobia. The employer needs to show a legitimate and clearly articulated "business necessity" (Del Valle, 2003, p. 151) for such rules, for example, that it would suffer "undue hardship" (Del Valle, 2003, p. 151) when employees speak foreign languages at work (Krahnke et al., 2003), for example, speaking a foreign language while on the radio in a police car or fire engine can cause confusion at the time of fighting a crime or a fire. Lacking such a business necessity, English-only in the workplace or otherwise seeking a linguistically homogenized work environment may be offensive and intimidating to Hispanics and other bilinguals, *mutatis mutandis,* not unlike the practice of slave owners intentionally mixing captured slaves who spoke different African languages to discourage the use of languages other than English on the Caribbean plantations (Holm, 1988).

In past years, several cases were decided in accordance with EEOC guidelines. For example, in *Martinez v. Lenox Health Care and Vencor, Inc.* (1999), a U.S. District Court in California ruled against an employer who created English-only rules in a nursing home. The Federal Court of the Northern District of Illinois, Eastern Division, settled a suit for eight former Hispanic plaintiffs brought against Watlow Batavia, Inc., for disciplining its workers for speaking Spanish with other co-workers on an assembly line (*EEOC v. Watlow Batavia, Inc.*, 1999). The District Court for the Northern District of Texas, Dallas Division, ruled against Premier Operator Services, Inc., in a lawsuit in which Spanish-speaking employees were fired after they refused to sign English-only agreements that would have stopped them from using Spanish in the workplace, including during breaks (*EEOC v. Premier Operator Services, Inc.*, 2000). The EEOC reached a landmark settlement against the University of Incarnate Word in San Antonio, Texas, for eighteen Hispanic housekeepers who were forbidden to use their native language of Spanish (*EEOC v. University of Incarnate Word in San Antonio,* 2001) (Krahnke et al., 2003). More recently, in a language discrimination case in Oklahoma (*Maldonado v. City Altus,* 2006), eleven Hispanic city street department employees of the City of Altus, a municipal corporation, alleged that the employer's English-only policy violated Title VII of the Civil Right Act of 1964 (Faingold, 2006). A previous ruling in favor of the employer who implemented the English-only policy was reversed. The Tenth Circuit Court held that a jury could reasonably find that the English-only policy had a discriminatory impact on Hispanic workers and that the trial court had erred in concluding that the employer had established a business necessity for the policy. The Tenth Circuit Court held that the policy itself, and not just the effect of the policy, in evoking hostility from the coworkers, contributed to the hostility of the work environment. By the end of 2006, the case was settled out of court in favor of the plaintiffs (City of Altus Council Meeting Minutes, October 3, 2006).

CODE-SWITCHING

Definition and Examples of Code-switching

Code-switching is "the alternate use of two or more languages in the same utterance or conversation" (Grosjean, 1982, p. 145). It has also been defined as "the use of two or more linguistic varieties in the same conversation (and) can be intra- or extra-sentential and also intra-word" (Myers-Scotton, 1990, p. 85). Poplack (2000) writes that "code-switching is the alternation of two languages within a single discourse, sentence, or constituent" (p. 221). Toribio (2001a) defines code-switching as "the ability on the part of bilinguals to alternate between their linguistic codes in the same conversational event" (p. 403). She writes that code-switching "may be inter-sentential or intra-sentential" (p. 404) and provides one example of each, in sentences (1a) and (1b) below, respectively (Spanish forms appear in italics. Slashes indicate language switches in the translations):

(1a) *Érase una vez una linda princesita blanca como la nieve.* Her stepmother, the queen, had a magic mirror on the wall.
Once upon a time there was a beautiful princess as white as the snow. / Her stepmother, the queen, had a magic mirror on the wall.
(1b) *Por la noche, los siete enanitos* found her on the ground, seemingly dead.
At night, the seven dwarfs / found her on the ground, seemingly dead.

Neurocognitive Basis for Code-switching

Grosjean (1997, 1998, 2001) found that bilinguals activate multiple "modes" unconsciously. Different language process mechanisms, representing the level of activation of each language at a given point in time, are activated according to such factors as language proficiency, attitudes, kinship relations, the setting (e.g., location, presence of monolinguals, degree of formality), and the stimuli (e.g., book read, TV program watched). When bilinguals interact with monolinguals, they behave in a monolingual language mode in that they are interacting with monolinguals of one or the other languages that they know. In contrast, when bilinguals communicate with other bilinguals, they find themselves in a bilingual mode with bilinguals who share their two languages and with whom they can code-switch. In this case, both languages are active but the one that is used as the base language, the main language of communication, is more active than the other. Grosjean's modes are supported by his own experiments and data as well as studies of code-switching among bilingual speakers of English and several immigrant languages in Australia (Clyne, 2003), English and Dutch in the Netherlands (Hermans,

Ormel, van Besselar, & van Hell, 2011), and English and Spanish in the United States (Canseco-Gonzalez, Brehm, Brick, Brown-Schmidt, Fischer, & Wagner, 2010).

In the bilingual mode, when bilinguals interact with others with whom they can code-switch, they use one language as the base for the production of an utterance while the other language serves as a guest language. When code-switching occurs, both topic and addressee, as well as the conceptual and pragmatic context, affect the activation of linguistic systems (Grosjean, 1997; Myers-Scotton & Jake, 2000). In such cases when code-switching is not appropriate, bilinguals are more likely to hesitate or produce linguistic errors. For example, bilinguals who code-switch often are obliged to use only one language, while at the same time they face competing lexicalized ideas in their first and second languages (i.e., in their L1 and L2) (Green, 1998).

Pioneering work by Green (1986, 1998) and his associates (Abutalebi & Green, 2007, 2008; Costa & Santesteban, 2004; Green & Abutalebi, 2013) suggests that languages can be at different levels of activation and that bilinguals can be influenced by the nature of a language that appears to be switched off. For example, in order to use one language (e.g., an L2) rather than another (e.g., an L1), the activation level of the L2 must exceed that of the L1. Speaking in one language rather than another results in the activation of that language but not in the total inhibition of the other (Green, 1998).

Neurocognitive experiments suggest that the brain exercises control on inhibitory mechanisms and relies on multiple neural regions to manage linguistic tasks such as code-switching (Abutalebi & Green, 2008). Inhibitory neurons implement controls on language selection and code-switching and manage competition between languages (Abutalebi & Green, 2007). Physiological resources are required to maintain control, and different regions of the brain are involved in output language selection (Abutalebi & Green, 2007). Code-switching involves the frontal-parietal-subcortical network. Specifically, it appears to take place in the basal ganglia. This is because of the basal ganglia's forward and backward connections to the prefrontal cortex which are involved in the types of cognitive control necessary to produce cognitive task switching such as updating, shifting, and inhibiting mental representations (Abutalebi & Green, 2008).

According to Abutalebi and Green (2008), even for fluent speakers of a second language who do not show performance errors in the production of linguistic structures, their linguistic repertoire (i.e., their L1 and L2) remains active at all times. This suggests that bilinguals must have the means to manage competition between languages in order to select the appropriate target language, for example, to use their L2 proficiently. The need to inhibit or suppress a non-selected language requires that bilingual speakers exercise cognitive control to avoid interference from the L1 and the production of errors (Green, 1986). Separation of L1 and L2 linguistic structures in the bilingual brain requires that structures in the language not in use be successfully inhibited to avoid interference (Costa & Santesteban, 2004; Green, 1986, 1998).

Further, and of particular importance for the aims of this chapter, neurocognitive evidence shows that there is a cognitive cost in making bilinguals suppress the use of their native language. Bilingual speakers must be able to put in some "cognitive effort" (Abutalebi & Green, 2007, p. 255) or carry a "cognitive load" (Green & Abutalebi, 2013, p. 524), which can lead to impaired linguistic performance due to linguistic interference, for instance, when going from the L1 to the L2 (Green & Abutalebi, 2013). The effort to avoid such interference can be extremely demanding because both the L1 and L2 are active in the brain during the production of linguistic structures in either of the languages available to the speaker. For example, in order to name an object in the less dominant L2, the more dominant L1 needs to be strongly inhibited, resulting in an increase in "persisting inhibition" (Abutalebi & Green, 2008, pp. 560-561) or control. While the nature of control can change with proficiency, functional imaging evidence obtained from lexical access tasks shows that there is still a switch cost and that persisting inhibition is important also for highly proficient bilinguals (Abutalebi & Green, 2008). There are constraints of time and energy (i.e., cost) because of competition between languages (Abutalebi & Green, 2007). Switching languages incurs a real cost, since the inhibition of the previously irrelevant language takes unnecessary processing time. For example, it takes longer to switch into a language that is more suppressed, especially for unbalanced bilinguals (Green, 1998).

Thus, in the bilingual brain, languages can be seen as resources that require energy to operate (Green, 1986). The most dominant language requires more active suppression and activation of inhibitory processes in the production of speech by bilinguals (Abutalebi & Green, 2007). As the evidence reviewed in this section suggests, requiring bilinguals to speak a non-native language at all times has a cost, literally, in neurocognitive terms.

Psycholinguistic constraints on code-switching

While we remember the content of conversations, it is very difficult to remember and repeat the exact words anyone has spoken. Bilinguals who are used to code-switching are often unaware of switching between languages. Code-switching takes place unconsciously. Speakers, including those who condemn code-switching, are unaware that they are switching from one language to another (Grosjean, 1982). Thus, bilingual speakers may not be aware of what language they are using at a particular moment in a conversation (Martinez, 2014). Bilinguals who regularly use more than one language may unconsciously code-switch or use more than one language to talk about the same subject. A good example of this was observed in a conversation among several bilinguals who code-switch frequently. At one point, according to Krahnke et al. (2003), the speakers were asked what language they had just used but they were unable to say. According to Lipski (1985), "speakers who engage in intra-sentential shifting (code-switching) are frequently unaware of having shifted well after the fact and may not be able to recall the exact moment of the shift, or to give justification for having changed languages in mid-stream" (p. 3).

According to some language theorists, code-switching can be considered an underlying syntactic mechanism, part and parcel of Chomsky's unconscious rule-governed linguistic competence (Chomsky, 1981, 2006; Pinker, 1994). For example, Toribio (2001b) and MacSwan and McAlister (2010) provide strong experimental evidence that code-switching can be used to support what theoretical linguistics call the "Functional Head Constraint," a formal principle of linguistic theory that permits constituent-internal code-switching in sentences such as (2a) and (3a) but prohibits such code-switching in sentences such as (2b) and (3b) (Spanish forms appear in italics; the asterisk means that a sentence is not well-formed, that is, that it is not something that bilinguals would be likely to say):

(2a) All of them *hablan español.*
They all speak Spanish (Toribio, 2001b).
*(2b) *Ellos han* completed degrees while working full time.
They have completed degrees while working full time (Toribio, 2001b).
(3a) *Mi hermano* bought some ice cream.
My brother bought some ice cream (MacSwan & McAlister, 2010).
*(3b) *El* bought some ice cream.
He bought some ice cream (MacSwan & McAlister, 2010).

In sentences (2b) and (3b) code-switching between the functional head in Spanish (auxiliary verb *han* "had" and article *el* "the") and their complement in English (verb-phrases "have completed" and "bought") produce ungrammatical structures which would be rejected as ill-formed Spanish/English code-switching by Hispanic bilinguals who code-switch. In contrast, sentences (2a) and (3a), where no code-switching occurs between functional head and complement, would be considered legitimate examples of Spanish/English code-switching.

Because Hispanic bilinguals code-switch in their attempt to fit in linguistically with their English-speaking coworkers and bosses, their code-switching becomes something that they do naturally and without awareness. Asking them not to code-switch seems to be, *mutatis mutandis,* not unlike asking black people to bleach their black skin in order to fit in with the white-skinned majority.

Sociolinguistic Constraints on Code-switching

In a conversation, the use of one or more languages may appear to be just a matter of choice for Hispanic bilinguals. Yet, Hispanic bilinguals feel obliged to use Spanish with Spanish-speaking relatives, teachers, friends, and others. To answer in English may be construed as an unfriendly gesture, or even dislike, by the addressee. Moreover, they feel constrained to have or show a positive attitude toward their native language (Faingold, 1999, 2004b). By the same token, language choice is also constrained by the social relationships among bilingual speakers participating in a conversation, that is, by the hierarchies found among speakers in the group (Palmer, 2009). Hispanic bilinguals of lower status may be obliged to answer in Spanish when spoken to in Spanish by other bilinguals of higher status; to answer in English may be considered an expression of disrespect (Krahnke et al., 2003). Similar considerations apply in the workplace. Here as well Spanish speakers feel that they must speak Spanish to other Spanish speakers to avoid disrespecting them.

For Spanish-speaking Hispanics in the United States, as well as other ethnic groups such as blacks, Italians, and Jews, there is a vital connection between language and ethnicity (Labov, 1978). In addition, as Fishman, Gertner, Lowy, and Milán (1986) note, "since language is the most elaborate symbol system of humankind, it is no wonder, then, that particular languages become symbolic of the particular ethnocultures in which they are embedded and which they index" (p. xii). More than fifty years ago Haugen (1956) noted that language "is at once a social institution, like the laws, the religion, or the economy of the community, and a social instrument which accompanies and makes possible all other institutions. As an institution it may become a symbol of the community group" (p. 87). Similarly, as Grosjean (1982) writes, "it is a well-accepted notion among sociolinguists that language is not just an instrument of communication. It is also a symbol of social group identity, an emblem of group membership and solidarity" (p. 117). Code-switching is used by bilinguals to claim membership in multilingual communities (Anzaldúa, 1987). Among U.S. Hispanics, code-switching in conversation with other Hispanics is construed as a friendly act (Faingold, 2004b; Zentella, 1997).

Mexican Americans, the largest Spanish-speaking group in the United States, as well as the other U.S. Hispanic minorities, "are extremely attached to their language and culture and have no problems in retaining them. The region they live in once belonged to them, as the Spanish place names remind them; they often return to Mexico to visit relatives, newcomers to the States arrive almost daily, many TV and radio stations broadcast in Spanish . . . " (Grosjean, 1982, p. 101; see also Faingold,

2012a, 2014). As Lipski (1985) puts it, "this type of language shifting (code-switching), which is characterized by a smooth flow between Spanish and English, is common in most U.S. Hispanic communities, and has even become an identifying characteristic of much of Hispanic-American literature in the United States" (p. 3).

In summary, based on the neurocognitive, psycholinguistic, and sociolinguistic evidence available, one can ascertain that code-switching between Spanish and English among U.S. Hispanics has, literally, a cognitive cost and is not a matter of choice but an unconscious and unintentional linguistic behavior as well as a crucial marker of social and cultural identity for these individuals or groups.

Monolingual English speakers often overlook the difficulty that non-native speakers of English have in expressing themselves in English, a language in which they may be fluent but not native (Grosjean, 1982). Krahnke et al. (2003) note that the vocabulary of speakers of Spanish and other languages may be limited to culturally specific topics of conversation, for example, the family, a child's behavior, or health issues, or because of the complexity of the issue, such as legal and financial matters. They may not find it possible to talk about these topics in English because they simply do not have the language proficiency to do so. Thus, non-English speakers may be confronted either with not talking about some subjects or trying to do so in English and risk a communication breakdown. Lacking a business necessity, English-only rules may be intimidating and offensive to Hispanic and other bilingual individuals or groups because such rules prevent them from doing something that is natural and culturally relevant to them.

III

Language Rights in the Southwest of the United States

FIVE

Language Rights in the Southwest of the United States and the Treaty of Guadalupe Hidalgo

Several indigenous minorities inhabit the United States and its territories. One indigenous minority is the Mexican American, who trace their lineage to the Mexicans who were living in the American Southwest at the time of annexation by the United States of more than half of the Mexican territory (this includes the states of Arizona, California, Nevada, New Mexico, Utah, and parts of the states of Colorado, Kansas, Wyoming, and Oklahoma). Other indigenous groups include Puerto Ricans, American Indians, native Hawaiians, Samoans, the Chamorro people of Guam and the Northern Mariana Islands, and the Carolinians of the Northern Mariana Islands (Faingold, 2017). Although from time to time some of them have raised the issue of independence, especially in Puerto Rico, they generally have been content with signing treaties that granted them some degree of autonomy or special rights within the United States. With the exception of the Mexican Americans of the Southwest, all of the conquered minorities mentioned above have obtained special powers of self-government, including language rights. For example, in both the State of Hawaii and Guam, the indigenous languages, Hawaiian and Chamorro respectively, have co-official status with English. Similarly, in Puerto Rico, Spanish and English are co-official languages (Faingold, 2017; Kilty & Vidal de Haymes, 2000; Kymlicka, 1995).

It was not for lack of trying that Mexican Americans failed to obtain language rights in the Southwest. The historical record demonstrates that since the beginning of the occupation of the Southwest, Mexican Americans fought to obtain language rights for Spanish-speakers. For example, in 1848 in California, Mexican Americans succeeded in passing a constitutional measure to have all state laws and regulations translated into Spanish. But only a few years later, in 1855, the California legislature refused to provide for the translation of laws into Spanish (Weber, 2003).

In New Mexico, because Mexican Americans were numerically dominant, they successfully opposed public schools and opted instead for parochial schools, where Spanish was the language of instruction. Thus, in 1890 Mexican Americans in New Mexico voted strongly against statehood because a new constitution threatened the parochial school system. In 1912, when New Mexico gained statehood and its 1910 constitution took effect, Spanish speakers obtained the constitutional right to vote, hold public office, have access to bilingual teachers, and sit on juries regardless of their ability to speak, read, or write in English. The Mexican Americans of New Mexico succeeded in making these language rights permanent because at the time of enactment the New Mexico constitutional assembly made these provisions difficult to amend.

On the other hand, in Arizona and Texas, Mexican Americans, who were numerically inferior and consequently lacked political power, were not even able to produce language legislation to protect their right to use Spanish in public (Weber, 2003).

A consensus exists that the language rights of Mexican American speakers of Spanish in the Southwest are protected by the Treaty of Guadalupe Hidalgo (henceforth, the Treaty). This idea has been accepted not only by leading scholars of the Treaty (e.g., Flores & Murillo, 2001; Martinez-Brawley & Zorita, 2001; San Miguel & Valencia, 1998) but also by important Mexican American activists (e.g., Lopez Tijerina, 2000; Rendon, 1971) and influential theorists in language policy (e.g., Kymlicka, 1995).

This chapter argues that those who argue that the language rights of Mexican Americans in the southwestern states of the United States are protected by the Treaty are mistaken. I demonstrate that a close reading of the Treaty reveals that it cannot be used in an American court of law to protect the linguistic rights of Spanish speakers living in southwestern states of the United States or elsewhere. This is because the text of the Treaty, as ratified by both the United States and Mexican governments, makes no mention of civil rights, or even language or culture rights. Thus, I submit that the Treaty is not the correct legal instrument to argue in favor of linguistic rights for Spanish-speakers in the United States. Rather, more sound arguments can be made under more modern civil rights legislation, such as Titles VI and VII of the Civil Rights Act of 1964 (Faingold, 2006, 2011, 2012a, 2012b, 2016a).

VIOLATIONS OF AND MODIFICATIONS TO THE TREATY OF GUADALUPE HIDALGO

Article 7 of the Treaty of Guadalupe Hidalgo granted U.S. citizenship to Mexican Americans living in the Southwest at the time of annexation. But a large part of the population in the annexed territories included Mexican Americans who had Indian ancestry, and in violation of the Treaty these individuals were not given U.S. citizenship, nor did they receive the constitutional protections of Article 7 of the Treaty, which were automatically given to all Mexican Americans of European ancestry living in the annexed territories (Meeks, 2007).

> Article 7
> Those who shall prefer to remain in the said territories may either retain the title and rights of Mexican citizens, or acquire those of citizens of the United States. But they shall be under the obligation to make their election within one year from the date of the exchange of ratifications of this treaty; and those who shall remain in the said territories after the expiration of that year, without having declared their intention to retain the character of Mexicans, shall be considered to have elected to become citizens of the United States.
> In the said territories, property of every kind, now belonging to Mexicans not established there, shall be inviolably respected. The present owners, the heirs of these, and all Mexicans who may hereafter acquire said property by contract, shall enjoy with respect to it guarantees equally ample as if the same belonged to the United States. (Treaty of Guadalupe Hidalgo, Article 7)

In California the Indian tribes were deprived of the protections specified in the Treaty, and they became the victims of murder, slavery, and starvation. Their population declined by more than 100,000 in twenty years as white people overran their tribal lands and committed genocide. Moreover, many Mexican Americans guaranteed American citizenship under the Treaty had Indian ancestry or were dark skinned. In a unanimously adopted proviso at the first meeting of the California legislature in 1848, the new California constitution restricted suffrage to white citizens exclusively (Wilson Moore, 2003). Similarly, in the Territory of New Mexico, where most of the Indian population lived, citizenship was limited to white people until statehood in 1912 (Griswold del Castillo, 1990). As early as 1863, the Arizona legislature limited voting rights to "white men and white Mexican men," thereby excluding Mexican Americans of Indian ancestry (Glenn, 2002, p. 159). In these ways, within a generation of the Treaty, Mexican Americans in the annexed territories became a disenfranchised, poverty-stricken minority (Anna, 1993; Griswold del Castillo, 1990).

Soon after the Treaty's ratification, the U.S. legal system was used to violate whatever meager protections the Treaty provided to protect the property and civil rights of Mexican Americans in the territories. Local laws were deemed to supersede the Treaty (Griswold del Castillo, 1990). Most importantly, the Supreme Court, in violation of the U.S. Constitution (Article 6, Section 2; Article 3, Section 2, Clause 2), which gives international treaties that have been ratified by the U.S. Senate and the president of the United States the same status as the Constitution, incorrectly claimed that U.S. laws take precedence over international treaties. As a result, the Treaty was not enforced when the property and civil rights of Mexican Americans were at stake.

The intent to deny rights to Mexican Americans living in the territories was evident even as the Treaty was being ratified. For instance, Article 10 protected land grants made by Mexico to its citizens in the annexed territories but was entirely stricken by the U.S. Senate during the ratification process.

> Draft of Article 10 before Ratification
> All grants of land made by the Mexican Government or by the competent authorities, in territories previously appertaining to Mexico, and remaining for the future within the limits of the United States, shall be respected as valid, to the same extent that the same grants would be valid, if the said territories had remained within the limits of Mexico. (Griswold del Castillo, 1990, pp. 180–181)

That the Treaty was modified to deny property rights to Mexican Americans holding land grants in what is today the Southwest of the United States comes as no surprise because the U.S. Army effectively was occupying more than half of Mexico, including Mexico City, at the time. And yet the United States was following its own legislation to the letter since according to the U.S. Constitution (Article 2, Section 2, Clause 2), the president of the United States has the right to negotiate treaties which must be confirmed by the U.S. Senate. Most important, the U.S. Senate has the power to amend a treaty, and strike and change articles at will.

Mexico could have refused to ratify the Treaty after the U.S. Senate amended it, but the Mexican government chose to ratify it. Obviously, Mexico had little choice in the matter. The Treaty was in fact a *diktat*, rather than a negotiated agreement between equals, as indicated by the fact that during negotiations, the U.S. Army was occupying most of Mexican territory, including Mexico City, the nation's capital.

The deletion of Article 10 created chaos among Mexican American holders of land titles in California, resulting in promulgation of the Federal Land Act of 1851, which opened Mexican American lands to litigation in American courts. Thus, as a result of fraud, manipulation, and indebtedness, nearly 40 percent of the land held by Mexican Americans in California before 1840 was transferred to American ownership, forcing marginalized Mexican Americans into wage labor and, ultimately, poverty (Wilson Moore, 2003).

Similarly, when the draft of Article 9, which aimed to protect the civil rights of Mexican Americans, was submitted to the U.S. Senate for ratification, the words "civil rights" were replaced by the word "religion" and the phrase "admitted as soon as possible" was replaced by the expression "at the proper time." Also, at the time of ratification, the U.S. Senate deleted from Article 9 of the draft Treaty legal wording granting Mexican Americans political rights equal to those obtained by French and Spanish citizens in Louisiana and Florida in the aftermath of the Louisiana Purchase from France (1803) and the Adams-Onis Treaty with Spain (1819), respectively. Clearly, to paraphrase George Orwell, for the U.S. Senate, in the treaty-making process, some nations were more equal than others.

> Draft of Article 9 before ratification
> The Mexicans who, in the territories aforesaid, shall not preserve the character of citizens of the Mexican Republic, conformably with what is stipulated in the preceding Article, shall be incorporated into the Union of the United States, and admitted as soon as possible, according to the principles of the Federal Constitution, to the enjoyment of all the rights of citizens of the United States. In the meantime, they shall be maintained and protected in the enjoyment of their liberty, their property, and the civil rights now vested in them according to the Mexican laws. (Griswold del Castillo, 1990, pp. 179–80)

> Article 9
> The Mexicans who, in the territories aforesaid, shall not preserve the character of citizens of the Mexican Republic, conformably with what is stipulated in the preceding article, shall be incorporated into the Union of the United States and be admitted at the proper time (to be judged of by the Congress of the United States) to the enjoyment of all the rights of the citizens of the United States, according to the principles of the Constitution; and in the meantime, shall be maintained and protected in the free enjoyment of their liberty and property and secured in the free exercise of their religion without restriction. (http://www.ourdocuments.gov/doc.php?doc=26&page=transcript)

Not surprisingly, Mexican historians have used the Treaty of Guadalupe Hidalgo to argue that the United States purposely violated the civil rights of Mexican Americans in the annexed territories. A study of the Mexican War and the Treaty of Guadalupe Hidalgo by the well-known Mexican historian Gastón García Cantú notes that the Mexican government at the time was deeply concerned about the rights of its citizens remaining in the United States. He notes that Mexican diplomats at the time of signing the treaty were very much aware that the destiny of thousands of its citizens in the United States would be discrimination and contempt, but the Mexican diplomats had no means to stop the Americans from violating the rights of Mexican Americans in the annexed territories (García Cantú, 1971).

LANGUAGE RIGHTS AND THE TREATY OF GUADALUPE HIDALGO

A close reading of the Treaty reveals that neither Article 9 (see above), nor any of its articles, are designed to protect the linguistic rights of Mexican Americans in the territories annexed by the United States after the Mexican-American War. That is, the text of the Treaty, as ratified by both the United States and Mexican governments, makes no mention of civil rights, let alone language and culture rights.

Nevertheless, there is broad consensus among scholars of the Treaty of Guadalupe Hidalgo that Spanish speakers in the Southwest are protected by it, especially by Article 9. For example, San Miguel and Valencia (1998, p. 362) misquote from the Treaty when they argue that the right of Spanish speakers to maintain their language through bilingual education, and the right to use Spanish in public are protected by Article 9 of the Treaty:

> The subtraction of Spanish from public education was accomplished through the enactment of English-language policies at the state and local levels, which not only prescribed English as the medium of instruction in the schools, but also discouraged, inhibited, or prohibited the use of Spanish...They also violated the Treaty of Guadalupe Hidalgo, which guaranteed Mexican Americans "the enjoyment of all the rights of citizens of the United states," *including the right to maintain their language* (emphasis added). (San Miguel & Valencia, 1998, p. 362)

Freeman (1975, p. 26) admits that "the treaty does not explicitly refer to either culture or language;" yet, without offering any arguments to support his claim, he states that "the Treaty of Guadalupe Hidalgo can be interpreted as *protecting the colonists' and their descendants' use of Spanish* (emphasis added)." Similarly, Flores and Murillo (2001, p. 202) state, also without offering any arguments to support their claim or citations from the Treaty, that "the Treaty of Guadalupe Hidalgo . . . *accorded to protect the language rights* of Mexicans living in the newly annexed and conquered territories of the U.S. Southwest (emphasis added)." Similarly, Rendon (1971, p. 71) states that "culture, *language* (emphasis added) and religion" are rights due to Mexican Americans under the Treaty. In the same vein, Martinez-Brawley and Zorita (2001, p. 59) argue that the "Treaty of Guadalupe Hidalgo guaranteed the right of the former Mexican citizens to *maintain their culture and, by extension, their language* under the flag of the USA (emphasis added)."

Finally, and most importantly, the consensus that the Treaty protects the language rights of Mexican Americans in the Southwest has made its way to authoritative language policy works. Thus, for example, Kymlicka (1995, p. 12) mistakenly states that "language rights were also guaranteed to Chicanos (Mexican Americans) in the south-west under the 1848 Treaty of Guadalupe Hidalgo."

In spite of the fact that the Treaty of Guadalupe Hidalgo, as we have seen, lacks the necessary legal language to protect the language rights of Mexican Americans in the United States, in *Tijerina v Henry* (1969), using the Treaty as a legal instrument, Reies Tijerina brought a class-action lawsuit against New Mexico's State Board of Education on behalf of poor Mexican Americans of Indian ancestry in the U.S. District Court of New Mexico. In his lawsuit, Reies Tijerina demanded a reapportionment (i.e., the redistribution of representation) of boards of education as well as the teaching of all classes in both English and Spanish (Lopez Tijerina, 2000). The District Court ruled against Reies Tijerina. In its ruling, the Court found that he had misinterpreted the scope of the Treaty when basing his suit for bilingual education on Articles 8 and 9 of the Treaty (see above). The Court ruled that the "Treaty between the United States and Mexico did not contemplate administration of public schools or confer any proprietary right to have Spanish language and culture preserved in public schools, and did not furnish basis for purported class action to have all subjects and all classes taught in both English and Spanish" (*Tijerina v Henry*, 1969).

In 1970, soon after the ruling by the District Court, Reies Tijerina appealed his case to the U.S. Supreme Court (398 U. S. 922 90 S. Ct. 1718). The Supreme Court dismissed the case, stating that the "Appellant's claim that the Treaty of Guadalupe Hidalgo specifies that a certain class of individuals are entitled under it to the preservation of their language and culture . . . is wholly unsubstantiated by the Treaty itself. Even if the Treaty read as Appellants wish it did, it could not, under any stretch of the imagination, be so construed" (398 U. S. 922 90 S. Ct. 1718).

In a dissenting opinion, Justice Douglas argued that, although the Treaty was not the right legal instrument in Reies Tijerina's case, the case could have merit on civil rights grounds, especially under the Thirteenth and Fourteenth Amendments to the U.S. Constitution (Faingold, 2012a).

As one expert in civil rights legislation explains, long after the signing of the Treaty,

> The Civil Rights Act transformed the legal landscape by outlawing discrimination and by creating legal remedies to battle discrimination. The Act enabled Mexican Americans to pursue a strategy both more likely to win substantive results and more likely to lead to cooperation with other minorities. . . . Civil rights legislation, enabled, for example, a new push for bilingual educational services (MacLean, 2007, pp. 125–130).

LANGUAGE RIGHTS FOR SPANISH-SPEAKERS IN THE UNITED STATES

The lack of linguistic protections in the Treaty does not mean that Mexican Americans and Spanish-speakers in general lack legal recourse to argue for language rights in the Southwest or elsewhere in the United States. Language discrimination cases have been argued using the U.S. Constitution and the Civil Rights Act of 1964 (see Faingold, 2006, 2011, 2012a, 2012b, 2016a, and references therein); the Voting Rights Act of 1965, which outlaws English literacy tests; the Bilingual Education Act of 1968, which was allowed to expire in 2002 under President George W. Bush; and Executive Order 13166, given by President Clinton in 2000 to federal agencies, which ensures that people who are LEP (limited English proficient) should have meaningful access to federally conducted and federally funded programs and activities.

A significant number of language discrimination cases have been won by Spanish speakers under Titles VI and VII of the Civil Rights Act of 1964. For example, in 1974 the Supreme Court held that school districts receiving federal funds have an obligation under Title VI of the Civil Rights Act of 1964 to assure that students are not excluded from meaningful participation in school programs on the basis of national origin.

Title VII of the Civil Rights Act has provided the grounds on which many language rights cases have been won. In 1999 a District Court in California ruled against Lenox Health Care and Vencor, who prohibited employees from speaking languages other than English in a nursing home. In 2000 a District Court in Texas ruled against Premier Operator Services for firing Hispanic employees who refused to sign an English-only agreement to prevent them from speaking Spanish at any time, including breaks. In 2000 the Federal Court in Illinois settled in favor of Hispanic employees of Watlow Batavia, which had disciplined workers for speaking Spanish with co-workers on an assembly line. In 2006 the 10th Circuit settled in favor of Hispanic employees of the City of Altus, Oklahoma, which had prohibited Hispanic employees from speaking Spanish at all times (Faingold, 2006, 2011, 2012a, 2016a).

CONCLUSION

As a result of the Mexican-American War (1846–1848), Mexico lost more than half of its territory to the United States through the Treaty of Guadalupe Hidalgo (1848). This chapter shows that the consensus among scholars of the Treaty and political scientists who study minority rights in the United States is that the language rights of Spanish-speaking Mexican Americans are protected by it, especially by Article 9. However, as this chapter shows, a close reading of the Treaty reveals that neither Article 9 nor any other article in it is designed to protect the linguistic rights of Mexican Americans in the annexed territories. Finally, the chapter argues that the Treaty of Guadalupe Hidalgo is not the correct legal instrument to protect the language rights of Mexican Americans, and that, instead, stronger arguments to protect the language rights of Spanish-speaking Hispanics, not only in the Southwest but in the United States as a nation, can be made under the U.S. Constitution and more modern civil rights legislation, such as Titles VI and VII of the Civil Rights Act of 1964.

SIX

Language Rights and Devolution in the Southwest of the United States

Devolution is the transfer of power from the central government of a sovereign country to a state, regional, or local government. This is usually achieved through the promulgation of statutes (e.g., the UK) or through changes in a country's constitution (e.g., Spain). Powers devolved to lower levels of government can be withdrawn at any time if no change of constitutional system has occurred (Burrows, 2000; Cole & Stafford, 2015; Faingold, 2016b; Tree, 2013). Also, since the early 1900s many states in the United States, including all the Southwestern states, with the exception of Texas, adopted Swiss-inspired democracy, the initiative and/or the referendum, to bring direct democracy to the states of Alaska (1959), Arizona (1911), Arkansas (1910), California (1911), Colorado (1910), District of Columbia (1977), Florida (constitutional initiative only) (1968), Idaho (1912), Illinois (constitutional initiative only) (1970), Kentucky (referendum only) (1915), Maine (1908), Maryland (referendum only) (1915), Massachusetts (1918), Michigan (1913), Mississippi (initiative only) (1992), Missouri (1908), Montana (1906), Nebraska (1912), Nevada (referendum only) (1904), New Mexico (referendum only) (1911), North Dakota (1914), Ohio (1912), Oklahoma (1907), Oregon (1902), South Dakota (1898), Utah (1900), Washington (1912), and Wyoming (1968). The initiative allows voters to propose a legislative measure (i.e., statutory initiative) or a constitutional amendment (i.e., constitutional initiative) by filing a petition bearing a required number of valid citizen signatures. The referendum refers a proposed or existing law or statute to voters for approval or rejection (Cronin, 1999). In this manner, by majority vote, a county, municipality, or similar sized area could set up its own linguistic regime, as in Switzerland's cantons, or as in coastal Finland, in which an area becomes or ceases to be bilingual when the number of speakers of a minority language in a census surpasses a certain benchmark, or when the percentages of minority language speakers decline (Kriesi & Trechsel, 2008; Linder, 2010). In multiethnic societies, devolution and direct democracy can be seen as ways to decrease regional linguistic, ethnic, or religious conflict. They have occurred in such diverse countries as Spain, Belgium, Switzerland, the UK, and Finland (Bartkus, 1999; Connolly, 2013; Tree, 2013).

This chapter argues that as with Catalan in Spain and Welsh in the UK, Spanish-speakers in the Southwest of the United States, and perhaps elsewhere in this country, could be subject to devolved language rights. All the Catalan, Welsh, and Hispanic peoples, who are indigenous to Catalonia, Wales, and the Southwest of the United States, respectively, were conquered and incorporated into a powerful neighbor, and currently have growing bilingual populations (Castro, 2013; Cole & Stafford, 2015; Faingold, 2012b, 2014, 2016b; Schmitt, 1984).

In the aftermath of the fusion of the crowns of Castile and Aragon that followed the alliance of the Catholic monarchs in 1469, Catalonia lost a great deal of political and military autonomy. Nearly two and half centuries later, in the aftermath of the War of Spanish Succession (1701–1714), in which Catalonia fought on the losing side against France and Spain, the use of Catalan by all state institutions, schools, courts, churches, and in book publishing, was banned. The Castilian language and its institutions would then dominate Catalonia for more than two hundred years, leading to the decline of Catalan (Davies, 2012).

In the second half of the nineteenth century, Catalan language and culture experienced a fast-paced process of recovery as a result of increasing Catalan nationalism and the political activities of its leading writers and politicians (Mar-Molinero, 2000). At the end of the Spanish Civil War (1936–1939), in which Catalonia again fought on the losing side, the use of Catalan and the production and public consumption of Catalan culture were prohibited by General Franco's dictatorship for more than forty years (Davies, 2012).

After Franco's death, Catalonia recovered most of its political autonomy, cultural institutions, and linguistic rights, with the enactment of a new Spanish Constitution in 1978, which devolved powers over a number of matters, including "the promotion of culture and research, and, where applicable, the teaching of the self-governing community's language (Article 17, Spanish Constitution, 1978), to Spain's autonomous regions." As a result, the use of Catalan grew rapidly in the autonomous region of Catalonia. A language training scheme was established to teach Catalan to civil servants who were expected to acquire a higher level of Catalan oral and written proficiency in order to earn promotion. This was the first step toward an ambitious revitalization project for the Catalan language which aimed to insure that it is spoken by government officials, to achieve active and literate bilingualism in the schools, to provide access to language training on demand for adults, and to motivate the population of Catalonia to participate in the recovery of the public use of the language (Wright, 1999).

In the aftermath of the Acts of Union of 1536 and 1542, which established English law for the administration of Wales, the English language became the sole official language of Wales, until the early twentieth century, when a process of resistance to Anglicization began to take place. This process took the shape of language revival movements dedicated to promoting the Welsh language for public use, especially in legal proceedings and the education system.

Since the formation of the Welsh Language Society in 1963, the struggle for language rights and equality between English and Welsh yielded significant results, especially in the availability of official bilingual forms and Welsh media, and in increasing access to the judicial system for monolingual speakers of Welsh (Williams, 2008). In 1964 the Labor Party won the general election in the UK; soon after it established the Welsh Office and a Secretary of State for Wales, which acquired responsibility for housing, local government and roads and, within a few years, for education and training, health, trade and industry, and the environment and agriculture.

In the mid-1990s, with labor back in power, the Welsh Language Act of 1993 was enacted by Parliament. At that point, language powers began to be transferred from the central government of the UK to the regional government of Wales. As a result, the people of Wales began a process of regaining recognition as a nation (albeit without territorial powers) with its own language, history, and flag. More importantly, Welsh people started gaining access to bilingual services, bilingual education, and protections against the predominance of English in public life (Huws, 2006; May, 2000). In 1997, a new referendum to decide the establishment of a Welsh Assembly, with the purpose of creating a far-reaching devolution scheme for Wales, took place, and by a narrow vote of 50.3 percent in favor, devolution became the law of the land in Wales. Within a few years, new linguistic priorities were set to establish language rights for speakers of Welsh, including the right of children to Welsh language education; the right to learn Welsh as an adult; the right to correspond in Welsh with public bodies; the right to receive information in Welsh from public bodies and certain private service providers; the right to use Welsh in a public meeting or inquiry; and the right to receive professional bilingual services from bodies approved by the Welsh Language Board (Williams, 2008).

DEVOLUTION IN THE SOUTHWEST OF THE UNITED STATES

Several indigenous minorities inhabit the United States and its territories. These include American Indians, Puerto Ricans, Hawaiians, and the Chamorro people of Guam and other Pacific island territories of the United States (i.e., speakers of Chamorro and Carolinian in the Commonwealth of the Northern Mariana Islands and Samoan in American Samoa) as well as Chicanos, the descendants of Mexicans who were left behind in the American Southwest in the aftermath of the Mexican American War (1846–1848) (Faingold, 2014, 2017; Fernández Asensio, 2014; Kymlicka, 1995; Porterfield, 2006; Sanchez, 1987; Shaffer, 2000).

The annexation of the Southwest was carried out through the Treaty of Guadalupe Hidalgo (1848) and the Gadsden Purchase (1854), which transferred the modern day states of Arizona, California, Nevada, New Mexico, Utah, and parts of the states of Colorado, Kansas, Wyoming, and Oklahoma to the United States (Faingold, 2014; Griswold del Castillo, 1990). At the time of annexation, the Spanish-speaking population of the Southwest was about 75,000, including 60,000 in New Mexico, 7,500 each in California and Texas, and 1,000 in modern-day Arizona. There were no permanent Mexican settlements in today's Nevada, Utah, Wyoming, Colorado, Kansas, Oklahoma, and Arizona above the Gila River (Weber, 2003).

With the exception of the Hispanics of the Southwest, all conquered indigenous groups in the United States and its territories have obtained special powers of self-government, including language rights. For example, in Puerto Rico, Hawaii, Guam, the Northern Mariana Islands, and American Samoa, the Spanish, Hawaiian, Chamorro, Carolinian, and Samoan languages are used in schools, courts, and other dealings with the government (Barreto, 2001; Faingold, 2017; Fernández Asensio, 2014; Sanchez, 1987; Shaffer, 2000; Willens & Siemer, 2002). In contrast, as we have seen, Hispanics in the Southwest did not obtain language rights at the time of annexation, since the annexation treaty, the Treaty of Guadalupe Hidalgo (1848), does not guarantee language rights for Spanish speakers in the Southwest (see chapter 5; Faingold, 2014). Also, as we have seen, arguments in favor of language rights for Spanish speakers can be made under the First and Fourteenth Amendments of the U.S. Constitution and the Civil Rights Act of 1964 (Del Valle, 2003; Faingold, 2012a, 2015, 2016a). The U.S. Constitution and the Civil Rights Act of 1964 protect individual rights, such as the right to free speech and the right of individuals not to be discriminated against based on their national origin (see chapter 4). However, in practice, language rights cases which have been litigated using these legal instruments have yielded contradictory results. This is because both the U.S. Constitution and the Civil Rights Act of 1964 lack a de jure definition of language as a protected class (Faingold, 2012a, 2016a). As we have seen, the United States needs to define the term "national origin" to cover "language" de jure by amending the Civil Rights Act of 1964, adding "language" to the protected categories "race, color, religion, sex, or national origin," since it is unclear as to what linguistic practices are covered by the term "national origin" (see chapter 3).

To protect the language rights of Spanish speakers in the United States it may be useful to explore legal options other than a constitutional amendment or a new act of congress. One such option would be a scheme to devolve language rights to cities and counties of the Southwest where the initiative and/or the referendum can be implemented legally and where Spanish speakers are a large part of the population. Devolution and direct democracy can provide mechanisms that could be used to produce real results in the area of language rights for minority speakers in the United States, similar to those implemented in Spain, the UK, and other countries as well as in some of the states (i.e., Hawaii, Louisiana, and New Mexico) and territories (i.e., Puerto Rico, Guam, the Northern Mariana Islands, and American Samoa) of the United States (Faingold, 2012b, 2017).

Devolution is not a new legal concept in the United States. Supporters of so-called states' rights have been advocating for the devolution of powers from Washington, D.C., to state and local governments for quite some time (Kymlicka, 1995). Arguments in favor of language devolution rights in the United States appear to be supported by Article 10 of the U.S. Constitution which states that "the powers not delegated to the United States by the Constitution, nor prohibited by it to the States, are reserved to the States respectively, or to the people." Moreover, since the U.S. Constitution does not declare any official languages or linguistic protections of any kind (Faingold, 2012a), there were not legal impediments for the establishment of language legislation for the protection of linguistic minorities by the states of Hawaii, Louisiana, and New Mexico (Faingold, 2012b) and by the U.S. territories of Puerto Rico, Guam, the Northern Mariana Islands, and American Samoa (Faingold, 2017).

The Constitution of New Mexico (1912) establishes provisions to protect the right to vote and hold office regardless of English speaking, reading, or writing ability (Articles 7, 21), access to bilingual education for children of Hispanic descent (Article 12), and the right to receive legal information in Spanish from the government (Article 20). However, these protections are not without problems or contradictions. Article 12, which provides for "the training of teachers in the normal schools or otherwise so that they (Hispanics) may become proficient in both the English and Spanish languages to qualify them to teach Spanish-speaking pupils and students in the public schools and educational institutions of the state" is contradicted by Article 21 which states that "schools shall always be conducted in English." The reason is that Article 12 provides for training teachers to become proficient in Spanish while Article 21 prohibits the use of Spanish in the schools. For what purpose would the state spend money and time training teachers to become proficient in Spanish if its use in the classroom is prohibited by law? Similarly, Article 20, which states that "all laws passed by the legislature shall be published in both the English and Spanish languages," was given a twenty-year expiration date. While Article 20 was renewed in 1931, and again for the last time in 1943, it was eventually dropped from New Mexico's constitution. In addition, funds were never appropriated to put Article 20 into practice (Genara Griego, n.d.). In spite of these problems and contradictions, the constitution of New Mexico offers far more language protections to Spanish speakers than any other state constitution in the United States. The linguistic protections provided by New Mexico's Constitution (1912) can serve as a source of inspiration for supporting the establishment of a language devolution scheme in the Southwest of the United States and perhaps elsewhere in this country.

Two questions remain. (1) Where in the Southwest can a language devolution scheme be put to a vote? (2) Why look to the Southwest, rather than other regions of the United States?

Regarding the first question, the obvious places for putting to the vote a devolution scheme, utilizing the initiative and/or the referendum, are congressional districts with the greatest concentration of Hispanics, which are found mostly in the southwestern states of Arizona, California, New Mexico, and Texas, in direct proximity to Mexico. Congressional districts in the Southwest where Hispanics constitute more than 33 percent of the population include Arizona districts 4 (63.9 percent) and 7 (56.0 percent); California districts 34 (78.7 percent), 38 (75.4 percent), 20 (70.4 percent), 43 (69.4 percent), 31 (68.2 percent), 47 (67.6 percent), 39 (66.5 percent), 32 (64.2 percent), 51 (62.4 percent), 28 (57.5 percent), 35 (54.5 percent), 18 (52.7 percent), 21 (51.2 percent), 17 (50.4 percent), and 35 (45.2 percent); New Mexico districts 2 (51.8 percent) and 3 (39.0 percent); and Texas districts 15 (82.5 percent), 16 (81.5 percent), 28 (78.9 percent), 29 (76.0 percent), 27 (73.2 percent), 20 (71.5 percent), 23 (66.4 percent), 32 (42.4 percent), and 19 (33.8 percent) (U.S. Census, 2010). The 33 percent benchmark is admittedly arbitrary. Accordingly, the threshold for approving a devolution scheme could be further lowered to 20 percent to include, for example, Arizona's district 2 with a Hispanic population of 20.8 percent (U.S. Census, 2010).

The right to receive devolution rights in states outside the Southwest may be appropriate at some point, especially in congressional districts with large Hispanic majorities, for example, districts 18 (66.95 percent), 21 (75.6 percent), and 25 (71.6 percent) in Florida; district 4 (73.5 percent) in Illinois; district 13 (50.6 percent) in New Jersey; and districts 12 (44.6 percent) and 16 (66.5 percent) in New York City (U.S. Census, 2010).

Further, likely targets for putting a devolution scheme to the vote are cities with high percentages of Hispanics, where politicians and bureaucrats responsible for welfare, education, health, and other social services are likely to recognize and provide bilingual services. As with congressional districts with the greatest concentration of Hispanics, cities with a high percentage of Hispanics are found in the southwestern states of Arizona, California, and Texas, in direct proximity to Mexico. For example, Phoenix, AZ (40.8 percent), Santa Ana, CA (78.2 percent), Salinas, CA (75.0 percent), Oxnard, CA (73.5 percent), Downey, CA (70.7 percent), Los Angeles, CA (48.5 percent), San Jose, CA (33.7 percent), San Diego, CA (28.7 percent), Laredo, TX (95.6 percent), Brownsville, TX (93.2 percent), McAllen, TX (84.6 percent), El Paso, TX (80.7 percent), San Antonio, TX (63.2 percent), Houston, TX (43.8 percent), and Dallas, TX (42.3 percent) are cities of the Southwest where Hispanics constitute more than 33 percent of the population (U.S. Census, 2010). Here as well the threshold for approving a devolution scheme has been lowered from 33 percent to 28.7 percent to include the city of San Diego, which the census identifies as a city with a large concentration of Hispanic residents (U.S. Census, 2010). Also, further discussions about devolution rights and bilingual services for Hispanics in cities outside the Southwest may be appropriate at some point, especially in cities with large numbers of Hispanic residents, for example, Chicago, and New York City, with 28.9 percent and 28.5 percent of Hispanic residents, respectively (U.S. Census, 2010).

Regarding the second question, the location of a devolution scheme in the United States, there are at least two reasons why devolution could start in the Southwest. First, as we have seen, the greatest concentrations of congressional districts and cities with Spanish-speaking majorities are found in the states of Arizona, California, New Mexico, and Texas. Second, like Native Americans, Puerto Ricans, Guamanians, and other inhabitants of the United States and its territories, the Hispanics of the Southwest are an indigenous minority with long historical roots in the region (De la Garza, Kruszewski, & Arciniega, 1972). Hispanic institutions and societies existed in the Southwest well before the Anglo settlers arrived. While they were defeated, conquered, and occupied, Hispanics in the Southwest never stopped fighting to protect the rights to their ancestral lands (De la Garza & Schmitt, 1986; López Tijerina, 2000), their cultural heritage (Gonzales, 2001; Haney Lopez, 2003; Hogan, 2014; Hunner, 2001; Marin, 2016; Weber, 2003), the use of their own language in the health system and other public services (Martinez, 2008; Sperling, 2009), and to receive a Spanish language education (Bale, 2011; Gándara & Orfield, 2012; Leckie, Kaplan, & Rubinstein-Avila, 2013; Mangual Figueroa, 2013; Palmer & Lynch, 2008; Valencia, 2008).

CONCLUSION

Devolution schemes and direct democracy in Spain, the UK, and other countries, combined with the study of linguistic protections provided in the constitutions and statutes of states in the United States and its territories offer insights for creating a language devolution scheme that could improve the language rights of Hispanics in the Southwest of the United States and perhaps also other areas of this country. The Catalan and Welsh experiences are of special interest for establishing a devolution scheme in the Southwest, since all the Catalan, Welsh, and the Hispanics of the Southwest are indigenous ethnic minority groups, who suffered conquest through armed struggle by a powerful neighbor from across the border, followed by social and economic displacement, while at the same time maintaining significantly distinct cultural values and identities, including their own language. Lessons learned from the study of diverse linguistic, legal, and political systems may produce a language environment more conducive to language rights for Spanish speakers in the United States (Faingold, 2012b, 2013, 2015, 2016b, 2017).

IV

Language Rights in the Pacific Island Territories of the United States

SEVEN

Language Rights in the United States Island Territory of Guam

In 1521, during the last leg of his circumnavigation of the globe, Magellan accidentally landed in Guam, a small island of 212 square miles at the southern tip of the Marianas Archipelago in the Micronesian region of Oceania (13.42113° N, 144.7397° E). In it, he encountered a native population, the Chamorro, which had remained isolated from the Western world for over 3,500 years (Cunningham, 1997; Lutz, 2010; Ridgell, 1997).

Until the arrival of the Jesuits to Guam in 1668, Spain had little or no interest in the native population of the island, which had decreased from 200,000 to 5,000, due to war and disease brought by the Spanish conquistadors (Natividad & Leon Guerrero, 2010). A real effort to colonize the island began in earnest with the Jesuits who came to impose Spain's mission of Christianizing the indigenous population of Guam, in a manner not unlike the colonization of Spanish America. In 1670, the Chamorro revolted against them and killed their leader, Father Diego Luis de San Vitores, but soon after, the Jesuits, who had arrived to Guam accompanied by Spanish soldiers, took back control of the island (Pesch, 1997; Sanchez, 1987).

Spain did not enact an official language policy to replace the use of the Chamorro language with Spanish throughout the Spanish colonial period. Instead, the Spanish missionaries learned Chamorro to govern the island. In the religious schools they established, Spanish was the language of instruction, prayer, and Biblical studies, but the education provided was mostly elementary and aimed to educate only a few individuals (Hewitt-Robertson, 1992) who were taught mostly "music" and "primary letters" (Carter, 1997, p. 182). By the end of Spanish rule, in the aftermath of the Spanish American War and the Treaty of Paris (1898), when the United States acquired Guam along with Puerto Rico and the

Philippines from Spain (Grabowski & Grabowski, 1992), Chamorro, a member of the Malayo-Polynesian branch of the Austronesian language family, was the dominant language of the island and Spanish was widely used as a second language (Sablan, 1997).

This chapter examines the language legislation of the United States territory of Guam in the Organic Act of Guam (1950) and its legal statutes, especially laws with provisions that protect the language rights of Chamorro-speakers, the native population of Guam. The chapter aims to aid the United States and its territories to improve the quality of language legislation. Lessons learned from studying Guam's language legislation can be of help for drafting and revising legislation that protects the language rights of minorities not only in Guam but also in other territories of the United States (e.g., the Commonwealth of the Northern Mariana Islands and American Samoa).

On August 7, 1899, Captain Richard P. Leary, the first American governor of Guam, arrived to the island and established the first naval administration (Carano & Sanchez, 1964). From then until the passage of the Organic Act of Guam (1950), the island "was governed much like a naval ship with a naval governor at the helm" (Natividad & Leon Guerrero, 2010, p. 2).

In Guam, the Americans encountered an indigenous population which had developed 75 percent literacy in Chamorro and 50 percent literacy in Spanish (Carano & Sanchez, 1964). Unlike the Spanish regime, the American military government enacted an official language policy with the explicit purpose of replacing the use of Chamorro and Spanish with English (Palomo, 1987). To this end, on January 22, 1900, Governor Leary issued General Order No. 12, Articles 1 and 4, which put education under the supervision and exclusive control of the U.S. Navy and imposed English as the sole language of instruction on the island. English, with emphasis in speaking skills and health education, became the most important subject of the curriculum in the schools (Carano & Sanchez, 1964).

> Article 1
> The system of public education in this island is hereby placed under the supervision and exclusive control of the Government, and all necessary expenses for the maintenance of the public schools will be defrayed by the Government.
>
> Article 4
> Instruction in the English language will be introduced in the public schools as soon as suitable teachers can be provided, and it is expected that the present force of native speakers will cheerfully and harmoniously cooperate with the teachers of English in order that the greatest benefits may be derived by both scholars and preceptors. (U.S. Navy Department, 1905, pp. 15-16, cited by Palomo, 1987, p. 21)

Yet, since there was a serious dearth of qualified English-speaking teachers on the island at the time, this order had little immediate impact (Carano & Sanchez, 1964; Carter, 1997; Underwood, 1987). In 1905, five years after Order No. 12 had been issued, English was being taught in the villages of Agana, Asan, Sumay, and Piti, while in the villages of Umatac, Merizo, and Inarajan children were taught by native Chamorro teachers in Spanish (Carter, 1997).

On January 23, 1900, Governor Leary issued General Order No. 13, which required that the adult Chamorro population learn to write their names in English precisely before July 1, 1900, and recommended that they learn to read, write, and speak English (Palomo, 1987; Thompson, 1947). On April 4, 1903, Governor William E. Sewell issued Order No. 54, which mandated that all leave applications must be written in English (Palomo, 1987). In 1906, Governor Templin M. Potts issued Special Order No. 17, which declared English the official language of the courts and other legal procedures (Clampitt-Dunlap, 1995). In 1917, Acting Governor Edward E. Simpson issued Order No. 243, which made English the only official language of the government and required that Chamorro be used only for official interpreting of the law (Thompson, 1947).

In the early 1920s, the U.S. Navy increased its English-only measures and made stringent changes to the school curriculum of the schools in Guam (Monnig, 2007). To this end, in 1922, Chamorro was banned in Guam's public schools and playgrounds. Students were reprimanded or penalized for speaking their native language. Speaking Chamorro was also prohibited on baseball fields. The implementation of these policies continued after the end of World War II, despite the fact that Chamorro remained the main language of communication of the island outside of the government and that most people in Guam spoke Chamorro better than English (Monnig, 2007; Sanchez, 1987).

The first American governors were aware that the indigenous population of the island spoke mostly Chamorro and to a lesser extent Spanish. They believed that creating a switch to English was necessary to govern the island effectively. "The General Orders, in essence, were the weapons employed to attain their goals" (Palomo, 1987, p. 24). The value of learning English was further promoted by Guam's first newspaper, the Guam Recorder, founded by the U.S. Navy in 1924. The newspaper, which was aimed at the general public, was written only in English (Sablan, 1997). In it, the American administration promoted negative attitudes toward the Chamorro language, with the purpose of increasing the rate of language shift from Chamorro to English:

> English will bring to the people of Guam, through the public schools, a knowledge of sanitation and hygiene, which will enable them to live in

> a correct manner. . . . Through English will come knowledge of fair play and a keen sense of honor. . . . With a knowledge of English under American tutorship will come a natural love for labor and industry by those who even come to think themselves as educated. (Guam Recorder, March 1924, cited by Sablan, 1997, p. 70)

Thus, in the first half of the twentieth century, English was aggressively promoted in the schools and in the workplace. Henceforth, the use of Chamorro in Guam decreased drastically as the U.S. Navy encouraged the use of English not only in the schools and at work, but also in the home. Since the American government provided most of the employment opportunities, work was mostly unavailable to those who lacked English language skills. Economic advancement became impossible without knowledge of English and parents began to use English at home to improve their children's chance of economic success (Clampitt-Dunlap, 1995; Sanchez, 1987).

In the mid-1950s, there was a focused effort to push the use of English in the schools even further. Some schools posted signs proclaiming that school campuses were "English-speaking areas." Many schools established a "Speak English Club" with a court to judge children who violated the English-only rules. Students who spoke only English at school received special recognition (Underwood, 1987, p. 230). "Children in American Guam were being deliberately weaned from their cultural roots by a school system that wanted them to be all that Americans were" (Underwood, 1987, p. 246). Not surprisingly, Chamorro women born in the aftermath of WWII (1945-1965) "identified Chamorro as their first language, (but) they also acknowledged that (Chamorro) had little use in situations beyond religious and home domains" (Santos-Bamba, 2013, p. 87). Women of the post-World War II generation, "made the conscious choice to prioritize and make English the language of their homes...by conversing with their children in English and using Chamorro only when upset or when they did not want their own children to understand adult conversation" (Santos-Bamba, 2013, p. 88). Their decision to exclude or limit Chamorro in the home comes as no surprise, since they grew up with an English-only policy that included "a provision that students who were caught using Chamorro in school were punished physically or through a demerit system . . . (that) devalued the significance of Chamorro language in their own lives" (Santos-Bamba, 2013, p. 91). Thus, as Santos-Bamba notes, "the use of Chamorro and English in these ways set in motion, for the next generation, the perception that English was for public and official domains and Chamorro language was reserved for private conversations or used as a language of reprimand" (2013, p. 88). Chamorro women of this generation "value English language and literacy as the vehicle to educational and professional advancement" (Santos-

Bamba, 2013, p. 88). Not surprisingly, as Santos-Bamba (2013) continues, "English dominates their life. . . . They use English with their children because they are better at English than Chamorro" (p. 92).

In the mid-1960s, the native intellectual elite of the island, which for sixty years had remained silent about the exclusion of the Chamorro language in government and the schools of Guam, began the first organized efforts to protect their native language. One of the first steps was the founding of the Chamorro Cultural Association of Guam. In 1964, the first annual lecture series was organized on the topics of preservation, familiarization, and the study of the Chamorro language, including preserving the unwritten traditions of the language and studying its grammar.

In the 1970s, a campaign to save the disappearing Chamorro language began with the approval of the island authorities (Clampitt-Dunlap, 1995). At that time, as a result of an increasing demand for Chamorro language instruction, the Chamorro Language and Culture Program was founded by Guam's government, with the explicit purpose of reviving and preserving Chamorro language and culture through the public school system (Underwood, 1987).

In the late 1980s and early 1990s, Guam's government became the Chamorro language principal defender. In 1987, it petitioned the U.S. Congress for commonwealth status, with the proviso that the Commonwealth Act must provide for the maintenance and preservation of the Chamorro language, culture, and traditions. In 1991, the University of Guam established the Micronesian Language Institute, to improve the teaching of Chamorro and other Micronesian languages, the production of language learning materials for teaching these languages, and the promotion of their appreciation in Guam and across Micronesia. In 1993, the University of Guam began to teach the first courses in Chamorro as part of a training program for Chamorro teachers (Clampitt-Dunlap, 1995).

In the late 1990s and early 2000s, Chamorro language and culture teaching was promoted throughout elementary, middle, and high schools across Guam. As of December 2016, a bill to develop a Chamorro language immersion pre-school program is awaiting Guam's legislative approval (KUAM News, December 13, 2016).

LANGUAGE RIGHTS IN THE ORGANIC ACT OF GUAM

In 1927, the United States granted citizenship to the inhabitants of the U.S. Virgin Islands, but failed to do the same for the people of Guam. In 1937, Congress took upon itself the task of granting citizenship to Guam's inhabitants. To this end, it introduced bills in both the House and the Senate to do just that, but these bills remained dormant for over a decade (Leibowitz, 1989).

On January 3, 1949, at the First Session of the 81st Congress in Washington, Senator Hugh Butler (R- Nebraska) reintroduced bill S. 185 for the establishment of a civilian government in Guam. At the same time, Delegate Joseph Farrington (R- Hawaii) reintroduced bill H.R. 391 to grant U.S. citizenship to the inhabitants of the island. Yet, despite these legislative efforts in the U.S. Congress, "officers in the field were holding back, and President Truman was losing Patience. It was time for more definite action" (Coulter Cogan, 2008, p. 152).

On February 2, 1948, in a special message to Congress on civil rights, President Truman announced:

> The present political status of our territories and possessions impairs the enjoyment of civil rights by their residents. I have in the past recommended legislation granting statehood to Alaska and Hawaii, and organic acts for Guam and American Samoa, including a grant of citizenship to the people of these Pacific islands. I repeat these recommendations. (Special Message to Congress by President Truman, February 2, 1948; cited by Coulter Cogan, 2008, p. 109)

On September 7, 1949, President Truman issued Executive Order 10,077, which transferred the administration of Guam from the Secretary of the Navy to the Secretary of the Interior. Soon afterward, the Navy and the Secretary of the Interior agreed on a date for the transfer to take place: July 1, 1950. At that time, the director of the Secretary of Interior's Division of Territories and Island Possessions ordered that on transfer day all naval personnel working for Guam's government would be replaced with natives of Guam. The order stated that if no qualified Guamanians were available, civilians from Hawaii or the mainland would be hired to replace all outgoing naval personnel.

On February 13, 1950, Congressman James Peterson (D- Florida) introduced bill H.R. 7273, the Organic Act of Guam, and on May 23 the House approved it (Coulter Cogan, 2008). On August 1, President Truman signed the bill into law. It was made effective retroactively from July 21, to celebrate the sixth anniversary of Guam's liberation from the Japanese occupation in World War II (Carano & Sanchez, 1964; Rogers, 1995).

The Organic Act of Guam (1950) regulates the relationship between Guam and the federal government. It serves all the purposes of a constitution, but, in contrast with a state constitution, the Organic Act obtains its powers from congressional action, not from the people of Guam who never voted on it. The U.S. Congress retained the power to amend the Organic Act or to enact new legislation concerning the island, a power that Congress does not have over a state (Leibowitz, 1989; Rogers, 1995).

The Organic Act declared that the new territory should be known officially as Guam, with Agana as the capital city and seat of government

(Carano & Sanchez, 1964). Section 3 of the Organic Act declared Guam to be an unincorporated organized territory. Unlike an incorporated territory (e.g., Alaska, Hawaii, Oklahoma, and other territories before acquiring statehood), an unincorporated territory is not considered to be an integral part of the United States (i.e., the U.S. Constitution does not apply, except as provided by the U.S. Congress). An unincorporated territory cannot become a U.S. state. That is, unlike Alaska, Hawaii, Oklahoma, and other states which were once territories, the Organic Act is not a preliminary step toward the admission of Guam into statehood (Faingold, 2017).

Molded after the U.S. government, Section 3 of the Organic Act provided for a territorial government with three distinct branches (i.e., executive, legislative, and judicial). Section 4 granted U.S. citizenship on all inhabitants of Guam born on the island after April 11, 1899, as well as their children and citizens of other countries resident on the island since April 11, 1899, excluding contract workers (mostly Filipinos) and others who had taken steps to maintain or acquire foreign nationality. Persons who were nationals of other countries and wished to retain their citizenship were allowed to do so, but they were required to declare, no later than two years after the establishment of the Organic Act, that they did not wish to become U.S. citizens (Rogers, 1995; Sanchez, 1987). Section 5 provided a Bill of Rights similar to that of the U.S. Constitution, with amendments guaranteeing freedom of religion, speech, and the press. It declared that no person may be deprived of life, liberty, or property without the due process of the law, and guaranteed the rights to peaceful assembly, to petition the government for redress of grievances, as well as the right to a speedy trial. It prohibited discrimination on account of race, language, color, or religion, and guaranteed equal protection under the law to all persons (Rogers, 1995; Sanchez, 1987).

In a novel legal approach that addresses language rights head-on, Section 5(n) of the Organic Act prohibits language discrimination de jure (see Faingold, 2004a, 2007, 2015, 2016b, 2017; see also Faingold, 2012a, 2012b, 2013, 2014, 2016a for de jure language hindering the language rights of minorities in the United States).

> Section 5(n)
> No discrimination shall be made in Guam against any person on account of race, *language* (emphasis added), or religion, nor shall the equal protection of the laws be denied. (Organic Act of Guam, 1950, Section 5(n))

In contrast, Title VII of the Civil Rights Act of 1964 was established by the U.S. Congress to protect several minorities (i.e., race, color religion, sex, and national origin) from discrimination, but language is not mentioned in it (Faingold, 2012a, 2015).

LANGUAGE RIGHTS FOR OFFICIAL LANGUAGES

Chapter 7, Sections 706 and 707, of the Government Code of Guam, established the official languages of the island, English and Chamorro.

> Section 706—Official Languages
> English and Chamorro are the official languages of Guam, provided, however, that the Chamorro language shall not be required for official recording of public acts and transactions.
>
> Section 707—English Version Controls
> Wherever there is found to exist a material difference between the English version and Chamorro version of any law or public document, the English version shall be held to be binding. (Government Code of Guam, Chapter 7, Sections 706 and 707)

According to Guam's official languages legislation, Chamorro is not required for recording public acts and transactions, and the only legally binding version of a law is found in the English text. Hence, Chamorro is of little or no practical use for official recordkeeping and/or the enactment of laws, since Guam's legal system does not require the use of Chamorro for the enactment of laws nor does it recognize the legality of texts written in Chamorro.

In 1980, Guam P.L. 15-147, Section 17402, established that signs displayed in public places must be written in English and Chamorro. The Chamorro Language Commission (see below) was charged with assisting in the translation of English signs and with approving all Chamorro signs.

> Section 17402
> Any permitted sign erected, displayed, or maintained . . . which contains a message in a language other than English or Chamorro in Roman alphabet characters shall contain a meaningful translation in English or Chamorro language which shall be printed on the sign using Roman alphabet characters. The Chamorro language Commission shall assist in translating and approve all Chamorro translations required by this Section for existing and new signs. The English or Chamorro translation must predominate the sign. (Guam P.L. 15-147, Section 17402)

Requiring bilingual English-Chamorro signs shows a willingness to accommodate the language needs of Chamorro speakers in Guam, albeit in a small and mostly symbolic manner.

LANGUAGE RIGHTS FOR CHAMORRO-SPEAKERS

The Chamorro Language Commission

In 1964, Chapter 7, Section 706, of the Government Code of Guam, established the Chamorro Language Commission, a government agency charged with protecting and developing Guam's indigenous language as a valuable resource for the people of Guam. Soon afterward, the Commission prescribed the production of a Chamorro grammar and a Chamorro-English dictionary.

> Section 706—Creation of Commission
> There is hereby established the 'Commission on the Chamorro Language,' to consist of five (5) members, all citizens of the United States and residents of Guam who must be conversant in the Chamorro language advise and consent of the Legislature for a term of three (3) years; provided, however, that of the members first appointed, one shall serve for one year, two for two years, and two for three years. (Government Code of Guam, Chapter 7, Section 706)

A decade later, the Commission produced a bill for the adoption of the original Chamorro names of towns and other places in Guam (Guam P.L. 17-10). The governor of Guam returned it to the legislature without its approval, but in 1983 the bill became law by legislative override. The same year, Guam P.L. 17-65, Article 4(a), established a policy for creating an official Chamorro language orthography.

> Article 4(a)
> The Chamorro Language Commission shall prepare a Chamorro Orthography and shall conduct a public hearing in Guam at least once in each of the four (4) legislative districts for the purpose of receiving comments and suggestions on the proposed orthography. Such Chamorro Language Orthography shall be available for public inspection at least ten (10) days prior to the scheduled public hearing. The date and subject matter of the scheduled public hearing shall be published in a newspaper of general circulation in Guam for three (3) consecutive days at least seven (7) days prior to the scheduled public hearing. (Guam P.L. 17-65, Article 4(a))

In 1992, Guam P.L. 21-121, Title 17, Section 46109(a), of the Government Code of Guam, created the Institute of the Chamorro Language within the Chamorro Language Commission.

> Section 46109(a)—Institute of the Chamorro Language
> This section creates the Institute of the Chamorro Language within the Chamorro Language Commission, which institute shall conduct instructional lessons in the Chamorro language, and give people the necessary vehicle for increasing their Chamorro speaking skills and their knowledge and understanding of the Chamorro language. (Guam P.L. 21-121, Title 17, Section 46109(a))

The Institute was charged with creating opportunities available to Guam's general population for learning Chamorro beyond the classroom. This law allowed the Institute to use funds allocated to the Commission and to charge fees for funding educational activities, hiring qualified teachers and administrators, and using government facilities, in addition to the Institute's own facilities, for the purpose of teaching Chamorro.

CHAMORRO IN EDUCATION

Section 1421g(b) of the Organic Act of Guam (1950), which gave the government of Guam authority over education, states that "The Government of Guam shall provide an adequate public educational system of Guam, and to that end shall establish, maintain, and operate public schools according to the laws of Guam (Organic Act of Guam, 1950, Section 1421g(b))." As per this law, in 1965, Guam's legislature passed Guam P.L. 8-71, the Education Autonomy Act, whereby the Department of Education (DOE) of the island was authorized to recruit personnel. The law also allowed the Business Office of the DOE to assume many of the functions previously held by the Department of Procurement and Supply (Underwood, 1987).

In 1973, Guam P.L. 12-31, Section 1168, authorized Guam's Board of Education "to initiate and develop a bilingual-bicultural education program (BBEP) emphasizing the language and culture of the Chamorro people." The purpose of this law was to revive and maintain Chamorro language and culture. The Board of Education noted at the time that "there is a definite need for students to learn and preserve that which is unique, while at the same time acquiring those attitudes and skills which are necessary for successful competition in the mainstream of American life" (Guam P.L. 12-31). The BBEP was charged also with improving spoken Chamorro proficiency on the island by allowing the use of Chamorro in content areas of language instruction as well as in class management in elementary and secondary schools, including the use of Chamorro-only instruction in the classroom or Chamorro-English bilingual techniques (Espinosa Indalecio, 1999).

In 1977, Guam P.L. 14-53, Sections 11682, 11684, and 11685, mandated the teaching of Chamorro language and culture in the public schools, the appropriation of funds for establishing a Chamorro Language and Culture Program, and creating programs for training educational employees with federal or local grants.

> Section 11682—Chamorro Language and Culture Courses Mandatory
> The Department shall include courses in Chamorro language and culture in its curriculum. Such courses shall be mandatory upon the development of a complete Chamorro Language and Culture Program but not later than the school year 1980 for all elementary students but elective for students in the junior and senior high schools.
>
> Section 11684—Receipt of Federal Funds
> The department is hereby authorized to continue receiving Federal funds for a Chamorro Language and Culture Program. . . . Appropriation of local funds is hereby authorized at any time that the federal assistance terminates.
>
> Section 11685—Staff Development
> A staff development program shall be established to include pre-service and in-service training of employees and the expansion of undergraduate and graduate courses in Chamorro language and culture at the University. This program shall be funded by either Federal or local grants, or both. (Guam P.L. 14-53, Sections 11682, 11684, and 11685)

In 1979, Guam P.L. 15-9 amended Section 11682 of the Government Code of Guam to mandate the teaching of Chamorro language to all children in kindergarten through second grade, with a grade to be added each year until the sixth grade, and elective classes for high school students; it mandated also the creation of a curriculum plan to teach these subjects.

> Section 11682—Chamorro Language and Culture Courses Mandatory (Amended)
> The department shall include courses in Chamorro language and culture in its curriculum. . . . [It] shall develop a comprehensive curriculum plan for instruction in the Chamorro language and culture to meet the needs of grades kindergarten through second grade, with a grade to be added each successive year until the sixth grade is included. . . . Elective courses for the secondary school shall be mandatory for all elementary students but elective for students in the junior and senior high schools. (Guam P.L. 15-9, Section 11682).

Following approval, a new educational policy was created. The new policy mandated 100 minutes of Chamorro instruction per week in kindergarten through the third grade and 150 minutes per week in the fourth and fifth grades. Guam's legislature appropriated the funds necessary to pay for this policy. The new policy focused on developing Chamorro language readers and other instructional materials and aimed mostly at improving Chamorro reading proficiency in elementary schools (Espinosa Indalecio, 1999).

In 1997, Guam's legislature noted a lack of textbooks, supplies, and classrooms for Chamorro classes in the public schools, especially in elementary schools. To remedy this situation, it enacted Guam P.L. 24-107, Title 17, Sections 8106 and 8107, which required that every public school must receive sufficient textbooks, supplies, and classrooms for Chamorro language and culture courses.

> Section 8106—Sufficient Textbooks and Supplies
> The Board shall provide textbooks adopted by the Board in sufficient quantities so as to assure that each student is assigned a textbook for the use of each student in each subject in which the student is enrolled and in which textbooks are used for classroom instruction, and such subjects shall include, but not be limited to, Chamorro Language and Culture.
>
> Section 8107—Chamorro Language and Culture Classroom(s) Required
> The Board shall require that every existing or new public school where new classrooms are constructed must provide sufficient classroom(s) for the exclusive purpose of Chamorro Language and Culture instruction, with a minimum of one (1) classroom designated for such use per school. For all other existing public schools, the Board shall immediately implement a study to determine the most feasible methods to provide sufficient classroom(s) for the exclusive purpose of Chamorro Language and Culture instruction, with a minimum of one (1) classroom designated for such use per school. (Guam P.L. 24-107, Title 17, Sections 8106 and 8107)

In 2011, Guam P.L. 31-45, Title 17, Section 8103(a), of the Government Code of Guam expanded the curriculum further by mandating explicitly that Chamorro language and culture course work be taught yearly in elementary, middle, and high school.

> Section 8103(a)
> The Department shall develop a comprehensive curriculum plan for instruction of the Chamorro language to be offered in all public elementary and secondary schools within Guam, in the following three (3) categories: Beginning Chamorro (Introduction to Chamorro Language); Intermediate Chamorro (Basic Usage and Application of the Chamorro Language); and Advanced Chamorro (Conversational Chamorro). The Department shall establish a program and require six (6) years mandatory course work in the Chamorro language and culture in the public elementary schools; mandatory course work in the Chamor-

> ro language and culture in the sixth (6th) grade in the middle schools, with the seventh (7th) grade to be included by School Year 2013-2014, and the eighth (8th) grade to be included to the program by School Year 2014-2015; and mandatory course work in the Chamorro language and culture in the ninth (9th) grade in the high schools, with the tenth (10th) grade to be included to the program by School Year 2014-2015. (Guam P.L. 31-45, Title 17, Section 8103(a))

Recently, in November 2016, Bill 398 was introduced to "appropriate $50,000 from the Tourist Attraction Fund to the Guam Visitors Bureau to print, purchase and distribute Chamorro literature . . . in Department of Education Schools" (KUAM News, November 15, 2016). A month later, a public hearing was held on Bill 399, to appropriate $150,000 for developing a Chamorro language immersion pre-school program (KUAM News, December 13, 2016). Since early 2017, Guam Department of Education is encouraging teachers to use social media for increasing the number of students learning to speak Chamorro, using Facebook or Instagram, posting audio or video files of students speaking Chamorro. Students using social media to post Chamorro phrases can earn prizes which are given to randomly selected submissions (*Pacific Daily News*, February 6, 2017). Also, as of March 2017, Chamorro language can be learned online at http://LearningChamorro.com. This website is free and offers a dictionary with about 12,000 Chamorro words, Chamorro lessons that teach words and phrases, an explanation of Chamorro sentence structure, basic conversations for the home, work, school, and other settings, and a media section with audio and video clips and real-life documents that can be used as learning tools. The Department of Education is also encouraging teachers to use the http://LearningChamorro.com website with social media together in the classroom (*Pacific Daily News*, March 13, 2017).

Thus, Guam established an impressive array of language laws with provisions to protect the language rights of Chamorro speakers in the areas of Chamorro language and culture education. First, in 1965, Guam's legislature passed the Education Autonomy Act, which allowed the Department of Education of the island to recruit personnel and to buy its own supplies. Later, in 1973, the legislature allowed the Board of Education to establish a bilingual-bicultural education program that, for the first time, infused the use of Chamorro in content areas of language instruction as well as in class management in elementary and secondary schools. The same year, using federal funds, the Department of Education started a Chamorro language and culture program in elementary schools. Four years later, the legislature mandated the teaching of Chamorro language and culture in public schools, appropriated the necessary funds to pay for it, and mandated the creation of opportunities for staff development. In 1979, the legislature mandated Chamorro language instruction to all children in kindergarten through sixth grade, and elective classes for high school students. In 2011, the legislature expanded the Chamorro language and culture curriculum further throughout elementary, middle, and high school. Recently, in December 2016, it introduced a bill to develop a Chamorro language immersion pre-school program. Since early 2017, the Department of Education is encouraging teachers to use social media and the internet to learn and speak Chamorro in the classroom and to teach about the culture of the island.

CONCLUSION

Unlike many states in the United States which declare English as the sole official language and/or have enacted provisions to protect official English (i.e., Alabama, Arizona, Arkansas, California, Colorado, Florida, Georgia, Idaho, Iowa, Kansas, Missouri, Montana, Nebraska, New Hampshire, North Carolina, Oklahoma, South Carolina, South Dakota, Tennessee, Utah, Virginia, West Virginia, and Wyoming) (Faingold 2012b), the territory of Guam did not declare English as the sole official language or establish provisions that hinder the rights of language minority groups (Faingold, 2017). As we have seen, Guam established language laws with provisions to protect the language rights of Chamorro speakers, the native population of Guam, especially in the areas of the Chamorro language and cultural education and language standardization. However, as noted, Chamorro is neither required for official recordkeeping nor for the enactment of laws, and is of little or no practical official use in Guam.

In spite of the impressive array of language laws enacted by Guam's legislature to teach Chamorro language and culture in the schools for more than half a century, the use of English continues to increase, while the use of Chamorro shrinks in Guam. The decreasing use of Chamorro in Guam seems to be due to a lack of indigenous Chamorro population buy-in of the importance of using the Chamorro language for the purpose of maintaining a modern-day Chamorro identity. While the Chamorro language is considered as worthy of protection by most people of Chamorro origin, it is not perceived by them as an essential component of a modern-day Chamorro identity (Clampitt-Dunlap, 1995). For example, a decade after the formation of the Commission on the Chamorro Language, in a study of language loyalty and ethnocentrism among college students of Chamorro origin, a little over two thirds of the respondents (67.72 percent) indicated that that they do not consider Chamorro language proficiency as essential to their Chamorro identity (Riley, 1975). Seven years later, a follow-up study confirmed that

> In spite of the emphasis given to ethnocentric awareness and the importance of the use of the indigenous language over the past seven

> years by the educational systems of the Territory, these students seem not to have been strongly impressed. As was pointed out in the earlier study, these students are still in the process of undergoing a cultural change, wherein their value system is slowly changing from a communal, traditional state to that of a civic, post-traditional state at least in the formal societal domains. (Riley, 1980, p. 332)

Given the long history of English-only policies that devalued the importance of the Chamorro language in Guam for decades, the increasing use of English at the expense of Chamorro should come as no shock. Not surprisingly, according to Guam's legislature, "the average number of proficient Chamorro speakers is over the age of 55. . . . With the average life expectancy of the Chamorro people, it's conceivable that the language will be extinct by 2025" (KUAM News, November 15, 2016). Unfortunately, this pessimistic outlook is supported by data from the last three U.S. Census statistics, which show the number of Chamorro speakers declining from 34,598 to 25,827 from 1990 to 2010; this negative outlook is further supported by recent data obtained from the U.S. Census Bureau showing that, between 2010 and 2016, the number of Chamorro speakers declined even further, bringing the number of speakers down to about a current estimate of 10,000 (*Pacific Daily News*, August 2016).

EIGHT

Language Rights in the United States Island Territory of the Northern Mariana Islands

The Northern Mariana Islands form a chain of fourteen small volcanic islands, located north of Guam, of which only three islands, about two-thirds of the total land area, are developed (i.e., Saipan, Rota, and Tinian). The majority of the population lives in Saipan, which is the largest and most developed of the archipelago. The other two are Rota and Tinian, which are less developed and have much smaller populations. Rota is used for small agricultural homesteads (Leibowitz, 1989). Most of Tinian has been taken over by the U.S. Armed Forces for military purposes (Broudy & Camacho, 2013), especially by the Marine Corps (Camacho, 2013).

The Spanish settled in the Northern Mariana Islands in 1668, at the same time they came to Guam. As in Guam, in the Northern Mariana Islands, the Spanish encountered a native population, the Chamorro (Willens & Siemer, 2002).

Unlike Guam, however, the Northern Mariana Islands were depopulated through a brutal policy of slaughter and forced resettlement of the Chamorro to Guam, which destroyed important traditional Chamorro practices in the Northern Mariana Islands (e.g., matrilineal clan land ownership traditions and navigational and boat-building skills, etc.). About a century and half later, in 1816, the Chamorro were permitted to return to the Northern Mariana Islands. The Chamorro who returned were educated in Spanish language schools established by the Catholic Church in which they studied reading, writing, arithmetic, music, and Catholic doctrine. Spanish colonial policy in the Northern Mariana Islands focused mostly on Christianizing the two indigenous groups, while the economic potential of the islands remained untapped during the Spanish period (Leibowitz, 1989).

The other group that inhabits the Northern Mariana Islands are the Carolinians, who arrived in several waves of migration between the early and mid-nineteenth century from a group of small coral atolls south of Guam, and "had a different language and tradition from the Chamorro majority" (Willens & Siemer, 2002, p. 35). For most of the nineteenth century, the Carolinians outnumbered the Chamorro; by the end of the 1800s, the demographic balance started to shift in favor of the Chamorro (Leibowitz, 1989); and, by the early 1970s, the Northern Mariana Islands were "about 75 percent Chamorro, 25 percent Carolinian" (Willens & Siemer, 2002, p. 309).

As in Guam, today the Chamorro constitute the dominant indigenous linguistic group of the Northern Mariana Islands. They speak Chamorro, a member of the Malayo-Polynesian branch of the Austronesian language family. Unlike the Chamorro, the Carolinians are culturally Truk and speak a variant of the Truk language (Chuukese), a member of the Micronesian branch of the Austronesian language family. Importantly, in contrast with the Chamorro, the Carolinians of the Northern Mariana Islands had no contact with the Spaniards, and, as a result, they tend to hold more Pacific Islander traditional views than the Chamorro, stressing community, heredity, and prestige over family and personal accomplishments (Hezel, 1983; Leibowitz, 1989).

This chapter examines the language legislation of the United States territory of the Commonwealth of the Northern Mariana Islands (henceforth CNMI) as stated in its constitution (1978) and legal statutes, especially laws with provisions that protect the language rights of Chamorro and Carolinian speakers, the indigenous peoples of these islands. The chapter aims to aid the United States and its territories to improve the quality of language legislation. Lessons learned from studying the language legislation of the CNMI can be of help for drafting and revising legislation that protects the language rights of minorities not only in these islands but also in other territories of the United States (e.g., Guam and American Samoa).

In the aftermath of the Spanish American War, at the time of the signing of the Treaty of Paris in 1898, in which the United States acquired the territories of Puerto Rico and Guam from Spain, *without having participated in the war,* the German Kaiser successfully concluded a secret agreement to purchase from Spain the Pacific islands not obtained by the United States at the time of negotiating the Treaty of Paris for the sum of $4,200,000, which included the Carolines, the Palau Islands, and the Northern Mariana Islands (Willens & Siemer, 2002).

Once the Germans assumed control of the Northern Mariana Islands, their main objective was to develop the islands by introducing a money economy, establishing copra plantations, encouraging commercial ventures, building roads, and providing health services. Importantly, public schools, where German was the language of instruction, were established, but the German language never took off in the brief period of German hegemony which came to an end in 1914, at the beginning of World War I, when the Japanese occupied the Northern Mariana Islands with the help of the British (Leibowitz, 1989).

In 1920, the Japanese were awarded a limited mandate in the Pacific under the League of Nations' supervision, which included the Northern Mariana Islands. Soon after, however, circumventing the League's rules, the Japanese established an administration to govern the Northern Mariana Islands as an integral part of Japan, with the purpose of colonizing them and exploiting their economic potential. Amazingly, in less than two decades, Japanese residents outnumbered the Chamorro and Carolinian combined populations. For example, by 1937, in the town of Garapan on the island of Saipan, Japanese residents came to outnumber all of the indigenous population of the Northern Mariana Islands five to one. The Japanese continued the economic development of the islands, establishing an important sugar industry, plantations of copra and coffee, commercial fishing, and phosphate mining. They improved social, health, and sanitation services, and built new schools with instruction in Japanese, but the Japanese language did not catch on with the native Chamorro and Carolinian population either during the Japanese period (Leibowitz, 1989).

After World War II, on July 18, 1947, the United Nations created a strategic-area trusteeship from former Japanese possessions, the Trust Territory of the Pacific Islands (TTPI), of which the United States assumed administrative responsibility (Ballendorf, 1984), until the Northern Mariana Islands became a territory of the United States in 1976 (Willens & Siemer, 2002) and the Federated States of Micronesia, the Republic of the Marshall Islands, and the Republic of Palau achieved independence a few years later (Faingold, 2017; Leibowitz, 1989). In 1951, the administration of the TTPI was transferred from the U.S. Navy to the Department of the Interior, but the Navy continued to rule it until 1962, when Interior took control of the Trust's administration.

On June 22, 1975, the population of the Northern Mariana Islands voted overwhelmly to become a territory of the United States, with 78.8 percent of the ballots cast in favor (Leibowitz, 1989), on a plebiscite in which the yes/no options on the forms appeared "with the Chamorro version first (*hunggan/ahe*), Carolinian second (*awer/ehe*), and English third (*yes/no*)" (Willens & Siemer, 2002, pp. 285–286). On July 1, President Ford informed the U.S. Congress about the desire of the people of the Northern Mariana Islands to sign the Covenant (Leibowitz, 1989). On July 21, 1975, after one day of hearings, the U.S. House of Representatives passed H.J. Res. 549 to grant Commonwealth status to the islands. On January, 27, 1976, after several months of hearings, deliberations, and amendments, the U.S. Senate voted in favor to adopt H.J. Res. 549. On March 24, 1976, President Ford signed H.J. Res. 549 Approving a Covenant to Establish a Commonwealth of the Northern Mariana Islands in Political Union with the United States, which made the Northern Mariana Islands an organized (i.e., governed by an organic act passed by the U.S. Congress or a territorial constitution passed with congressional approval) but unincorporated (i.e., the U.S. Constitution applies only partially) territory of the United States (Faingold, 2017; Willens & Siemer, 2002).

LANGUAGE RIGHTS FOR OFFICIAL LANGUAGES IN THE CNMI CONSTITUTION (1978)

As noted above, organized territories can be subject to an organic act passed by the U.S. Congress (i.e., the United States Virgin Islands and Guam), or they can have their own constitution, if it is passed with congressional consent (i.e., Puerto Rico and the CNMI). When a territory has its own constitution it is often referred to as "Commonwealth." Residents of these territories are citizens of the United States, and allowed to move to the mainland, but they cannot vote in federal elections. Each territory has a representative in the U.S. Congress, which cannot vote on the floor but may vote in committee (see chapters 2 and 7; Faingold, 2017; Leibowitz, 1989; Willens & Siemer, 2002).

Molded after the U.S. Constitution, the CNMI Constitution provides for a representative form of government (Article 5, CNMI Constitution, 1978), with separate Executive, Legislative, and Judicial Branches (Articles 2, 3, and 4, CNMI Constitution, 1978), and a Bill of Rights guaranteeing freedom of religion, speech, press, and assembly; due process, equal protection, and trial by jury; a clean and healthful environment; and the right to privacy (Article 1, CNMI Constitution, 1978). Also, as in the constitutions of many states in the United States, Article 9 of the CNMI Constitution adopted the trifecta of Swiss-inspired direct democracy (i.e., initiative, referendum, and recall) (see chapter 7).

However, as with the constitutions of Hawaii and American Samoa, the CNMI Constitution restricts the "acquisition of permanent and long-term interests in real property within the Commonwealth" to "persons of Northern Marianas descent" (Article 12, CNMI Constitution, 1978). To qualify as a "person of Northern Marianas descent," a person must meet two criteria: (1) the person must be a citizen or a national of the United States; and (2) the person must be at least one-quarter Northern Marianas Chamorro or Northern Marianas Carolinian blood or a combination thereof. For the purpose of determining descent under Article 12, a person is considered to meet the above criteria if he or she "was born or domiciled in the Northern Mariana Islands by 1950 and was a citizen of the Trust Territory of the Pacific Islands before the Termination of the Trusteeship with respect to the Commonwealth" (Article 12, CNMI Constitution, 1978).

Article 3, Section 301(a)-(c), of the CNMI Constitution, provides that the following persons and their children under the age of 18, who are not citizens or nationals of the United States under any other provision of law, and who on that date do not owe allegiance to any foreign state, become citizens of the United States:

> Article 3, Section 301
>
> (a) All persons born in the Northern Mariana Islands who are citizens of the Trust Territory of the Pacific Islands on the day preceding the effective date of this Section, and who on that date are domiciled in the Northern Mariana Islands or in the United States or any territory or possession thereof;
> (b) All persons who are citizens of the Trust Territory of the Pacific Islands on the day preceding the effective date of this Section, who have been domiciled continuously in the Northern Mariana Islands for at least five years immediately prior to that date, and who, unless under age, registered to vote in elections for the Mariana Islands District Legislature or for any municipal election in the Northern Mariana Islands prior to January 1, 1975; and
> (c) All persons domiciled in the Northern Mariana Islands on the day preceding the effective date of this Section, who, although not citizens of the Trust Territory of the Pacific Islands, on that date have been domiciled continuously in the Northern Mariana Islands beginning prior to January 1, 1974. (Article 3, Section 301, CNMI Constitution, 1978).

Article 22, Section 3, of the CNMI Constitution (1978), as amended in 1985, established the official languages of the island, Chamorro, Carolinian, and English.

> Article 22, Section 3
> The official language of the Commonwealth shall be Chamorro, Carolinian and English, as deemed appropriate and as enforced by the legislature. The legislature may provide that government proceedings and documents shall be in at least one of the three languages. This section shall not be subject to judicial review. (CNMI Constitution, 1978, Article 22, Section 3)

According to the CNMI's official languages legislation, Chamorro, Carolinian, and English can be used equally by the government and in legal proceedings. Unlike the territory of Guam, where "English and Chamorro are the official languages, provided, however, that the Chamorro language shall not be required for official recording of public acts and transactions" (Government Code of Guam, Chapter 7, Section 706), where the law requires that "the English version of any law or public document . . . shall be held to be binding" (Government Code of Guam, Chapter 7, Section 707), and where Chamorro is of little or no practical use in government transactions and in the courts (Faingold, 2017), the right to use the indigenous languages of the Northern Mariana Islands, Chamorro and Carolinian, in court are strongly protected rights in the CNMI.

The CNMI Supreme Court has consistently affirmed the right of indigenous Chamorro speakers to use their own language in court. For, example in a language discrimination case (*Commonwealth v. Deleon Guerrero*, 2003), Peter M. Deleon Guerrero, a Chamorro convicted of assault and battery by a trial court, asked the CNMI Supreme Court to overturn his conviction "on the grounds that the trial court did not allow him and his attorney to use the Chamorro language when conducting his trial and questioning witnesses" (*Commonwealth v. Deleon Guerrero*, 2003). He argued that the trial court's decision to prohibit the use of Chamorro in court "violated Article 22, Section 3, of the N.M.I. Constitution, which delineates Chamorro, Carolinian, and English as the official languages of the Commonwealth" (*Commonwealth v. Deleon Guerrero*, 2003). The appeal was based on a previous decision of the CNMI Supreme Court (*Jasper v. Quitugua*, 1999) which ruled that "native Chamorro-speaking people have a constitutional right to speak Chamorro in court" (*Commonwealth v. Deleon Guerrero*, 2003). While *Jasper* spoke very good English, he "was nonetheless entitled to speak Chamorro because the CNMI Constitution lists Chamorro as an official language" (*Commonwealth v. Deleon Guerrero*, 2003). Likewise, it deemed that Deleon Guerrero's "is a case involving Chamorro language, which is treated specially by the Constitution and this Court...(He) should have been allowed to conduct his trial in Chamorro, even though everyone involved spoke English perfectly well" (*Commonwealth v. Deleon Guerrero*, 2003). Thus, the CNMI Supreme Court ruled that Deleon Guerrero "had an absolute right to speak Chamorro during his trial. To hold otherwise would be to undermine Article 22, Section 3 of the N.M.I. Constitution" (*Commonwealth v. Deleon Guerrero*, 2003). The conviction was reversed and the case was remanded for a new trial. It is important to note, however, that in *Deleon Guerrero* the CNMI Supreme Court ruled also that residents of the Northern Mariana Islands do not have an absolute right to use Chamorro in court or in dealings with the government.

> Neither *Jasper* nor this decision creates an individual right to demand that government agencies conduct official business in all three lan-

guages. Rather, this principle applies only to court proceedings, as we have chosen to conduct our official business in this way. However, in choosing to conduct our business in this way, we hold that in order for the constitutional right to speak Chamorro or Carolinian to apply, the person who wishes to use these languages must be a native speaker of these languages. It would be too costly and time-consuming to allow everyone, regardless of their native language, to speak Chamorro and Carolinian. (*Commonwealth v. Deleon Guerrero*, 2003)

LANGUAGE RIGHTS FOR CHAMORRO AND CAROLINIAN SPEAKERS

The Chamorro and Carolinian Language Policy Commission

In 1982, CNMI P.L. 3–26, Sections 2 and 6(a)-(d), established the Chamorro and Carolinian Language Policy Commission, a government agency charged with the production of a Chamorro-Carolinian grammar, a Chamorro-Carolinian-English dictionary, and a standard orthography to be used in schools of the CNMI.

> Section 2—Establishment
> There is hereby established a Chamorro and Carolinian Language Policy Commission to consist of sixteen (16) members, eight Chamorros and eight Carolinians to be appointed by the Governor from nominations submitted by the director of the Bilingual/Bicultural Program and the Executive Assistant for Carolinian Affairs.
>
> Section 6—Duties
>
> (a) Study the antecedents, describe the grammar and prescribe good usages for the Chamorro/Carolinian language;
> (b) Prepare a modern and up-to date Chamorro/Carolinian/English dictionary;
> (c) Represent the Northern Mariana Islands in meetings and conferences on matters dealing with the Chamorro/Carolinian language; and
> (d) Make recommendation to the legislature on standard orthography to be used in schools. (CNMI P.L. 3–26, Sections 2 and 6)

In 2007, in the preamble of CNMI P.L. 15–229, the CNMI's legislature noted problems of language standardization, and a lack of competent translators of Chamorro and Carolinian, which was threatening the use of the two indigenous languages by the government:

> Certain official documents randomly translated in Chamorro or Carolinian by certain individuals were found to be inconsistent with the

> adopted Orthography and Dictionary of the Chamorro and Carolinian languages. This has created a division and difference of opinion among such translators. Therefore, there is a need to require Chamorro and Carolinian translators to become certified as competent and qualified translators...A Certification Committee on Chamorro and Carolinian Translators should be established (CNMI P.L. 15–229, Preamble)

To remedy this situation, in 2017, the CNMI's legislature enacted P.L. 15–229, Sections 1205(f)-(g) and 1206, which allowed the Language Policy Commission to establish new rules for the use of Chamorro and Carolinian. The new legislation required the creation of a Commission on Certification of Chamorro and Carolinian Translators and new rules for the use of Chamorro and Carolinian in government documents and public places.

> Section 1205—Chamorro and Carolinian Language Policy Commission: Duties and functions
>
> (f) Establish, formulate, and enforce policies for government and private sectors regarding Chamorro and Carolinian translations, and to certify all Chamorro and Carolinian translators;
> (g) Promulgate rules and regulations for Chamorro and Carolinian languages used on all government and public documents and public places including public buildings, roads, places, street naming, and private business signs;
>
> Section 1206—Committee on Certification of Chamorro and Carolinian Translators
> There is established within the Chamorro and Carolinian Language Policy Committee a Commission on Certification of Chamorro and Carolinian Translators comprised of three members of the commission. The commission shall adopt rules and regulations regarding the criteria, qualifications, and certification process of Chamorro and Carolinian translators.

In 2011, the CNMI's legislature completed the long-awaited finalization of the task of adopting an official Chamorro language orthography with the approval of CNMI P.L. 17–10.

> The Commission presented and explained the Standard Chamorro Language Orthography to the general public via Marianas Cablevision on the "Abiba I Lingguahi-ta" program; . . . the Commission adopted the Standard Chamorro Language Orthography on April 23, 2010. . . . On December 14, 2010, the Commission officially transmitted the Standard Chamorro Language Orthography to the seventeenth Northern Marianas Commonwealth Legislature for approval; . . . the Senate con-

> curring, that the seventeenth Northern Marianas Commonwealth Legislature hereby approves the Standard Chamorro Language Orthography. (CNMI P.L. 17–10)

Thus, CNMI's legislature produced significant language legislation for the promotion and use of Chamorro and Carolinian by the government and private sectors which allowed the Chamorro and Carolinian Language Policy Commission to establish new rules and regulations to "certify official translators for the Chamorro and Carolinian languages . . . formulating a unified procedure in translating the vernaculars to English" (*Saipan Tribune,* February 3, 2009); doing language surveys "to determine the types of programs needed to maintain and preserve these languages" (*Saipan Tribune,* September 15, 2004); offering Chamorro and Carolinian elective courses in elementary schools (*Saipan Tribune,* August 10, 2011); producing up-to-date Chamorro-English (*Saipan Tribune,* December 1, 2008) and Carolinian-English (*Saipan Tribune,* February 26, 2001; *Saipan Tribune,* March 26, 2005) dictionaries and a thorough revision of Chamorro orthography (*Saipan Tribune,* May 27, 2009); updating textbooks and classroom materials for teaching Chamorro and Carolinian in elementary schools (*Saipan Tribune,* August 10, 2011); producing computer-assisted instruction (*Saipan Tribune,* June 30, 2000) and automatic translation software (*Saipan Tribune,* September 1, 2005) in Carolinian, and multimedia materials such as the TV series "Finu'Chamorro" (*Saipan Tribune,* January 4, 2012) and the "Webisode" project Ketungu'Chamorro (*Saipan Tribune,* December 3, 2015) in Chamorro; offering free Chamorro conversation classes at the Joeten-Kiyu public library (*Saipan Tribune,* July 15, 2016); and participating in the Chamorro cultural festival at the California State University San Marcos (*Saipan Tribune,* February 26, 2016), the annual Chamorro language competition at the University of Guam (e.g., *Saipan Tribune,* March 12, 2005; *Saipan Tribune,* March 15, 2012; *Saipan Tribune,* March 23, 2017), the Chamorro and Carolinian language junior high and high school competitions organized by the CNMI (*Saipan Tribune,* June 9, 2011), and the Carolinian speech competition organized by the Carolinian Affairs Office (*Saipan Tribune,* October 10, 2016).

CONCLUSION

The CNMI's legislature enacted important language legislation, constitutional provisions and statutes that protect the language rights of the Chamorro and Carolinian indigenous population, especially in the areas of language use in the courts (e.g., *Commonwealth v. Deleon Guerrero,* 2003), by the government, and in language standardization.

However, the CNMI's legislature failed to establish language laws that might protect the maintenance and use of the CNMI's indigenous languages, Chamorro and Carolinian, in the schools. Only very recently, and perhaps too late to have any significant impact on the maintenance and use of Chamorro and Carolinian in the schools, House Bill 19–143, which mandates the teaching of Chamorro and Carolinian in public elementary, junior, and senior high schools throughout the islands, was introduced in the CNMI's legislature in early 2016 (*Saipan Tribune*, March 28, 2016). The bill required that "Chamorro and Carolinian must be used and spoken at all times in such classes" (*Saipan Tribune*, March 28, 2016) and that "the Public School System (hire) qualified or certified people to teach the languages, notwithstanding other requirements imposed by PSS for other teaching positions" (Radio New Zealand News, March 29, 2016).

It is doubtful whether the bill will have much impact in the maintenance and use of Chamorro and Carolinian in the schools, even if the legislature approves it, given that the CNMI Board of Education has already gone on record stating its opposition to mandated Chamorro and Carolinian teaching in the schools (*Guam Daily Post*, May 11, 2016). In an interview to the *Guam Daily Post*, Board of Education Chairperson Herman T. Guerrero stated:

> House Bill 19–143, which will require all public schools in the Commonwealth to teach Chamorro and Carolinian as a prerequisite to their students' graduation, is discriminatory. . . . If the legislature is really concerned about the local languages, then the bill should also apply to private schools. . . . And I'm sure the private schools are not in favor of that. . . . [The bill] will require hiring more teachers we don't have. . . . The Public School System should not be blamed if local children are not proficient in Chamorro and Carolinian. . . . Language really begins at home. . . . If the bill becomes law, many students would never graduate from high school. (*Guam Daily Post*, May 11, 2016)

A decade and a half ago, two prominent Pacific Islands scholars presciently noted that "both Chamorros and Carolinians, when faced with a pervasive and dominant American culture, might lose their distinctive languages and heritages as island peoples. The land alienation provision that restricted sales to outsiders was intended as a protective measure, but it might not work as intended" (Willens & Siemer, 2002, p. 345).

Not surprisingly, "preliminary findings of a survey conducted by the Chamorro and Carolinian Language Policy Commission in 2004 indicated that the use of indigenous languages—Chamorro and Carolinian—among elementary school students is at a very minimal percentage" (*Saipan Tribune*, August 7, 2004). "Only 15 percent of students in public schools speak the indigenous languages while the rest use the universal language, English, in and out of their households" (*Saipan Tribune*, January 27, 2009).

NINE

Summary, Conclusion, and Directions for Future Research

In this book, I have analyzed some of the U.S. federal, state, and territorial laws pertaining to the language rights of the inhabitants of the United States and its territories, especially minority language speakers, in the areas of political, legal, and educational access. I have provided a comprehensive analysis of language rights and the law in the U.S. Constitution and the Civil Rights Act of 1964, the constitutions of the fifty states, and the organic acts, constitutions, and statutes of the U.S. territories and the Freely Associated States. I have produced detailed case studies of the impact of language legislation on linguistic minorities in the Southwest of the United States and the U.S. Pacific island territories of Guam and the Northern Mariana Islands.

In chapter 1, I showed that U.S. states which are silent on language rights are consistent with the U.S. Constitution, while states adopting a "hands-on" legislation are in conflict with it, since the U.S. Constitution is silent about official languages and language legislation. I showed that, with the exception of California, Hawaii, Louisiana, and New Mexico, which enacted language laws that protect the linguistic rights of minorities, states adopting a hands-on language legislation that aims to protect the official language (i.e., English) without enacting language provisions to protect linguistic minorities in their constitutions and/or statutes are deemed to be "nativist" because they seem unfavorable toward speakers of minority languages. Similarly, in chapter 2, an exhaustive screening of the constitutions, organic acts, and statutes of the territories of the United States and the Freely Associated States showed that, with the exception of the American Virgin Islands, which do not declare any official languages or language provisions in its constitution and statutes, the territories and associated states enacted "hands-on" language legislation and policies that seem beneficial to minority groups. Unlike many of the states in the United States discussed in chapter 1, which declare English as the sole official language and/or enact provisions to protect official English without enacting language legislation to protect linguistic minorities in their constitutions and/or statutes, none of the territories and associated states declares English as the sole official language or establishes provisions that hinder the rights of language minority groups.

In chapter 3, I showed that neither the U.S. Constitution nor the Civil Rights Act of 1964 define de jure obligations of the United States toward members of language minorities and that, as a result, they often fail to protect linguistic minorities from discrimination by proponents of English-only and official English legislation. I postulated that a revised civil rights legislation is more likely to help solve conflicts by defining legally the status of speakers of languages other than English in the United States. In this vein, chapter 4, pushed to the limit state-of-the-art theories of psycholinguistics, neurolinguistics, and sociolinguistics as evidence that the use of a second language can be unconscious and automatic; that using a non-native language can have a cost in neurocognitive terms; that the Spanish language can be a crucial marker of social and cultural identity for Hispanics; and that, lacking a business necessity, rules that prohibit the use of a language other than English at all times in the workplace can constitute a civil rights violation.

In chapter 5, I took a fresh look at the Treaty of Guadalupe Hidalgo, which formalized the annexation of the Southwest to the United States in 1848, and debunked the long-held consensus among scholars of the Treaty that the language rights of Hispanics in the Southwest are protected by it. I showed that a close reading of the Treaty reveals that it was not designed to protect the linguistic rights of Hispanics in the Southwest. Instead, the language rights of Hispanics are more likely to be protected by the U.S. Constitution and the Civil Rights Act of 1964 (but see chapter 3 for problems found in these two major pieces of legislation). As I show in chapter 6, a devolution scheme, inspired by those established in Spain and the UK, might help protect the language rights of Spanish-speakers in congressional districts and cities with the greatest concentration of Hispanics, especially in the Southwest, in direct proximity to Mexico.

In chapter 7, I studied language legislation enacted in the United States territory of Guam and showed that, as in a few states in the United States, such as those discussed in chapter 2 (i.e., California, Hawaii, Louisiana, and New Mexico), Guam established language laws with provisions that protect the language rights of the native Chamorro-speaking population, especially in the areas of education and language standardization. Yet, as I also show in this chapter, the use of English in Guam is increasing, while that of Chamorro is shrinking, due to the lack of buy-in of the importance of speaking Chamorro for the purpose of maintaining a modern-day Chamorro identity. Similarly, in chapter 8, I studied the language legislation of the Commonwealth of the Northern Mariana Islands. Unlike Guam, this territory failed to establish language laws that might protect the language rights of its indigenous minorities (Chamorro and Carolinian) in the schools, but it enacted strong constitutional provisions that protect the language rights of Chamorro and Carolinian-speakers in the courts (something that, as we have seen, Guam's legislation failed to do). As in Guam, the use of English is increasing, while the use of indigenous languages is shrinking in the Northern Mariana Islands, which may be due to a lack of support for the teaching of Chamorro and Carolinian in the schools by both the legislature and the Board of Education of the Northern Mariana Islands.

In chapter 2, I offered a comprehensive and systematic analysis of the language legislation of all the territories and associated states of the United States. In chapters 7 and 8, I produced detailed case-studies of language rights in the territories of Guam and the Northern Mariana Islands. Yet, for a number of reasons, detailed case-studies of language rights and the law in the territories of Puerto Rico, the United States Virgin Islands, and American Samoa were left out of this book.

The politics of language education and language use in Puerto Rico deserve more time and space than I could offer in this work (Algren de Gutiérrez, 1987; Barreto, 2001; Clampitt-Dunlap, 2000; Schmidt, 2014; Torres González, 2002; Tucker, 2005; Vélez, 2000). New research might confirm that Spanish in Puerto Rico is not under attack (e.g., Spanish has remained the basic language of instruction of the island since 1948) (Crawford, 2000). Importantly, future research might show that recent bilingual legislation has made Spanish even more resilient to attacks from mainland U.S. English (i.e., Chapter 5, Title 1, Sections 59, 59(a)-(c), and 60, of the Laws of Puerto Rico Annotated [2013], which codify Spanish and English as co-official languages of Puerto Rico, and require that official Spanish and English translations of written texts and oral interpretation of government and legal proceeding be available [Section 59(a)], that competent interpreters and translators be employed [Section 59(b)], that "no public or private document shall be annulled on account of being written in one or the other of the official languages of Puerto Rico" [Section 59(c)], and that both languages are valid for issuing all licenses and certificates, including drivers' licenses, marriage licenses, and professional qualification certificates [Section 60)]).

> Section 59—Spanish and English; Official Languages
>
> Spanish and English are established as official languages of the Government of Puerto Rico. Both languages may be used, indistinctively, in all departments, municipalities or other political subdivisions, agencies, public corporations, offices and government dependencies of the Executive, Legislative and Judiciary Branches of the Common-

> wealth of Puerto Rico, pursuant to the provisions of §§ 59–59f of this title, or by that which is provided by a special law.
>
> Section 59(a)—Translations and Interpretations
> When necessary, written translations and oral interpretations shall be made from one language to the other so that the interested parties can understand any proceeding or communication in said languages.
>
> Section 59(b)—Employment of Interpreters and Translators
> The departments, municipalities or other political subdivisions, agencies, public corporations, offices and government dependencies of the Executive, Legislative and Judiciary Branches of the Commonwealth of Puerto Rico shall employ competent interpreters and translators, when necessary, to carry out the provisions of §§ 59–59f of this title.
>
> Section 59(c)—Documents
> No public or private document shall be annulled on account of being written in one or the other of the official languages of Puerto Rico, pursuant to the provisions of §§ 59–59f of this title, or by that which is provided by a special law.
>
> Section 60—Licenses and Certificates; Issuance in Both Official Languages
> The Secretaries of the Department of Transportation and Public Works, the Department of Health and the Department of Education are hereby directed to amend the regulations so that driver's licenses, marriage licenses, and the various professional qualification certificates issued by the Department of Education, among others, of the directors and teachers be issued in both official languages of the Government of the Commonwealth of Puerto Rico.

Due to the paucity of up-to-date scholarly information on the language policy situation in American Samoa, a detailed study of language rights in the territory must await future research (Baldauf, 1984, 1990; Huebner, 1986; Mülhäusler, 1996; Wallace, 1964). New research might show whether Samoans continue to be afraid that the English language "will destroy their traditional language and culture" (Baldauf, 1990, p. 273); whether "although the children are taught English in school, at home they speak only their own Samoan language" (Wallace, 1964, p. 167); whether "the Samoan language has remained strong, especially in personal usage situations" (Baldauf, 1990, p. 273); and whether Samoans continue "(to cling) tenaciously to their language, the receptacle and unifying agent of their Polynesian culture" (Wallace, 1964, p. 167). A study of the impact of Article 1, Section 3, of the Constitution of American Samoa (1967), which "(protects) persons of Samoan ancestry against alienation of their lands and the destruction of the Samoan way of life and *language* (author's emphasis)," might reveal whether American Samoa's constitution has made the Samoan language more or less resilient to attacks from mainland U.S. English.

> Article I, Section 3—Policy Protective Legislation
>
> It shall be the policy of the Government of American Samoa to protect persons of Samoan ancestry against alienation of their lands and the destruction of the Samoan way of life and language, contrary to their best interests. Such legislation as may be necessary may be enacted to protect the lands, customs, culture, and traditional Samoan family organization of persons of Samoan ancestry, and to encourage business enterprises by such persons. No change in the law respecting the alienation or transfer of land or any interest therein shall be effective unless the same be approved by two successive legislatures by a two-thirds vote of the entire membership of each house and by the Governor.

As with American Samoa, due to the dearth of scholarly information, a study of language rights in the American Virgin Islands must await future answers (Dookhan, 1994). As in the U.S. mainland, the absence of an explicit language policy in its organic act and statutes has not prevented the American Virgin Islands from practicing implicit language policies that promote the use of English (e.g., in government operations, such as the courts and the educational system), while also backing the use of Spanish in the community, for example, by providing bilingual programs that serve thousands of Puerto Rican students in public schools (Leibowitz, 1989). Future studies might reveal whether the American Virgin Islands have become more (or less) tolerant toward immigrant Spanish-speakers from Puerto Rico and elsewhere in Latin America.

References

Abutalebi, J., & Green, D. W. (2007). Bilingual language production: The neurocognition of language representation and control. *Journal of Neurolinguistics, 20,* 242–275. doi: 10.1016/j.neuroling.2006.10.003

Abutalebi, J., & Green, D. W. (2008). Control mechanisms in bilingual language production: Neural evidence from language switching studies. *Language and Cognitive Processes, 23,* 557–582. doi: 10.1080/01690960801920602

Administrative Policy # 1.13. (2002). City of Altus, Oklahoma.

Alexander, N. (2004). The politics of language planning in post-apartheid South Africa. *Language Problems and Language Planning, 28,* 113–130. doi: 10.1075/lplp.28.2.02ale

Algren de Gutiérrez, E. (1987). *The movement against teaching English in schools of Puerto Rico.* Lanham, MD: University Press of America.

Anna, T. E. (1993). Demystifying early nineteenth-century Mexico. *Mexican Studies / Estudios Mexicanos,* 9, 119–37. doi.org/10.2307/1052103

Anzaldúa, G. (1987). *Borderlands/la frontera: The new mestiza.* San Francisco, CA: Aunt Lute Books.

Baldauf, R. B. (1982). The language situation in American Samoa. *East-West Center Institute Language Planning Newsletter,* 8, 1–8.

Baldauf, R. B. (1990). Education and language planning in the Samoas. In R. B. Baldauf, & A. Luke (Eds.), *Language planning and education in Australasia and the South Pacific* (pp. 259–273). Clevedon, UK: Multilingual Matters.

Bale, J. (2011). The campaign for Spanish language education in the "Colossus of the North," 1914–1945. *Language Policy, 10,* 137–157. doi: 10.1007/s10993–011–9200–0

Ballendorf, D. A. (1984). American Administration in the Trust Territory of the Pacific Islands 1944 to 1968. *Asian Culture Quarterly, 12,* 1–10.

Ballew, G. (2006). *Court allows challenge to City's "English-only" policy.* Retrieved from http://www.laborlawyers.com.

Barreto, A. A. (2001). *The politics of language in Puerto Rico.* Gainesville, FL: University Press of Florida.

Bartkus, V. O. (1999). *The dynamic of secession.* Cambridge, UK: Cambridge University Press.

Broudy, D., & Camacho, L. (2013) 'Sweetening' the Pentagon's deal in the Marianas: From Guam to Pagan. *The Asia-Pacific Journal: Japan Focus, 11.27,* 1–20. Retrieved from http://apjjf.org/2013/11/27/Daniel-Broudy/3963/article.html

Brown-Blake, C. (2006). Fair trial language and right to interpretation. *International Journal of Minority and Group Rights, 13,* 391–412. doi: 10.1163/157181106779848368

Burnaby, B. (1996). Language policies in Canada. In M. Herriman & B. Burnaby (Eds.), *Language policies in English-dominant countries* (pp. 159–219). Clevedon, UK: Multilingual Matters.

Burrows, N. (2000). *Devolution.* London, UK: Sweet & Maxwell.

Camacho, L. (2013). Poison in our waters: A brief overview of the proposed militarization of Guam and the Commonwealth of the Northern Mariana Islands. *The Asia-Pacific Journal: Japan Focus, 11.51,* 1–18. Retrieved from http://apjjf.org/2013/11/51/Leevin-Camacho/4050/article.html

Cameron, D. R., & Krikorian, J. D. (2008). Recognizing Quebec in the constitution of Canada: Using the bilateral constitution amendment process. *University of Toronto Law Journal, 58,* 389–420. doi: 10.1353/tlj.0.0010

Canseco-Gonzalez, E., Brehm, L., Brick, C. A., Brown-Schmidt, S., Fischer, K., & Wagner, K. (2010). Carpet or carcel: The effect of age acquisition and language mode on bilingual lexical access. *Language and Cognitive Processes, 25,* 669–705. doi: 10.1080/01690960903474912

Carano, P., & Sanchez, P. C. (1964). *A complete history of Guam.* Rutland, VT: Charles E. Tuttle Company.

Carter, R. R. (1997). Education in Guam to 1950: Island and personal history. In L. D. Carter, W. L. Wuerch, & R. R. Carter (Eds.), *Guam history: Perspectives, volume 1.* (pp. 181–218). Mangilao, Guam: University of Guam.

Castro, E. (2013). *What's up with Catalonia? The causes which impel them to separation.* Barcelona, Spain: Catalonia Press.

Chomsky, N. (1981). *Lectures on government and binding.* Dordrecht, Netherlands: Foris.

Chomsky, N. (2006). *Language and mind.* Cambridge, UK: Cambridge University Press.

City of Altus Council Meeting Minutes. (2006, October 3). Retrieved from http://altusok.gov/sites/default/files/ccfiles/CC100306.pdf.

Civil Right Act of 1964. Retrieved from http://usinfo.state.gov.usa/info/laws/majorlaw/civilr19.htm.

Clampitt-Dunlap, S. (1995). *Nationalism, native language maintenance and the spread of English: A comparative study of the cases of Guam, the Philippines and Puerto Rico* (Unpublished Doctoral Dissertation). University of Puerto Rico Rio, Piedras, PR.

Clampitt-Dunlap, S. (2000). Nationalism and native-language maintenance in Puerto Rico. *International Journal of the Sociology of Language,* 142, 25–34. doi: 10.1515/ijsl.2000.142.25

Clyne, M. (2003). *Dynamics of language contact: English and immigrant languages.* Cambridge, UK: Cambridge University Press.

Cole, A., & Stafford, I. (2015). *Devolution and governance: Between capacity and constraint.* Houndsmills, Basingstoke, UK: Palgrave Macmillan.

Connolly, C. K. (2013). Independence in Europe: Secession, sovereignty, and the European Union. *Duke Journal of Comparative & International Law, 24,* 51–105. Retrieved from http://scholarship.law.duke.edu/cgi/viewcontent.cgi?article=1396&context=djcil.

Costa, A., & Santesteban, M. (2004). Lexical access in bilingual speech production: Evidence from language switching in highly proficient bilinguals and L2 learners. *Journal of Memory and Language, 50,* 491–511. doi: 10.1016/j.jml.2004.02.002

Coulter Cogan, D. (2008). *We fought the navy and won: Guam's quest for democracy.* Honolulu, HI: University of Hawai'i Press.

Crapo, W. (2006). *Are English-only policies discriminatory?* Retrieved from http://www.woodcrapo.com.

Crawford, J. (2000). *At war with diversity: U.S. language policy in an age of anxiety.* Clevedon, UK: Multilingual Matters.

Cronin, T. E. (1999). *Direct democracy: The politics of initiative, referendum, and recall.* Cambridge, MA: Harvard University Press.

Cunningham, L. J. (1997). The ancient Chamorros of Guam. In L. D. Carter, W. L. Wuerch, & R. R. Carter (Eds.), *Guam history: Perspectives, volume 1* (pp. 11–36). Mangilao, GU: University of Guam.

Davies, N. (2012). *Vanished kingdoms: The rise and fall of states and nations.* New York, NY: Penguin Group.

De la Garza, R. O., & Schmitt, K. (1986). Texas land grants and Chicano-Mexican relations: A case study. *Latin American Research Review, 21,* 123–138.

De la Garza, R. O, Kruszewski, Z. A., & Arciniega, T. A. (1972). *Chicanos and Native Americans: The territorial minorities.* Englewood Cliffs, New Jersey: Prentice Hall.

Del Valle, S. (2003). *Language rights and the law in the United States: Finding our voices.* Clevedon, UK: Multilingual Matters.

Dookhan, I. (1994). *A history of the Virgin Islands of the United States.* Kingston, Jamaica: Canoe Press.

Du Plessis, T. (2000). South Africa: from two to eleven official languages. In K. Deprez & T. du Plessis (Eds.), *Multilingualism and government* (pp. 95–110). Pretoria, South Africa: Van Schaik.

Espinosa Indalecio, A. R. (1999). *Policies and practices of Chamorro cultural narratives in the community and schools of Guam* (Unpublished doctoral dissertation). University of Arizona, Tucson, AZ.

Faingold, E. D. (1999). The re-emergence of Spanish and Hebrew in a multilingual adolescent. *International Journal of Bilingual Education and Bilingualism, 2,* 283–295. doi: 10.180/13670059908667695

Faingold, E. D. (2004a). Language rights and language justice in the constitutions of the world. *Language Problems and Language Planning, 28,* 11–24. doi: 10.1075/lplp.28.1.03fai

Faingold, E. D. (2004b). *Multilingualism from infancy to adolescence.* Greenwich, CT: Information Age Publishing.

Faingold, E. D. (2006). Expert witness report. Code-switching in the workplace. Maldonado v. City of Altus, 433 F. 3d 1294 (10 Cir. 2006).

Faingold, E. D. (2007). Language rights in the 2004 draft of the European Union Constitution. *Language Problems & Language Planning, 31,* 25–36. doi: 10.1075/lplp.31.1.03fai

Faingold, E. D. (2011). Code-switching in the work-place: The linguistic rights of Hispanics in the United States. Comisión de Lingüística (Eds.). *Comunicación Social en el Siglo XXI, volume 1* (pp. 107–11). Santiago de Cuba, Cuba: Centro de Lingüística Aplicada.

Faingold, E. D. (2012a). Language rights in the United States Constitution and the Civil Rights Act of 1964. In P. C. Miller, J. L. Watzke, & M. Montero (Eds.), *Readings in language studies, volume 3: Language and identity* (pp. 447–457). Grandville, MI: International Society for Language Studies.

Faingold, E. D. (2012b). Official English in the constitutions and statutes of the fifty states in the United States. *Language Problems and Language Planning, 36,* 136–148. doi: 10.1075/lplp.36.2.03fai

Faingold, E. D. (2013). Official English in the constitutions and legislative statutes of the 50 states in the United States. Presented at the 19th International Congress of Linguists. Geneva, Switzerland. July 22–27, 2013.

Faingold, E. D. (2014). Language rights for Mexican Americans and the Treaty of Guadalupe Hidalgo. In P. C. Miller, J. L. Watzke, & M. Montero (Eds.), *Readings in language studies, volume 4: Language and social justice* (pp. 271–281). Grandville, MI: International Society for Language Studies.

Faingold, E. D. (2015). Language rights in the European Union and the Treaty of Lisbon. *Language Problems and Language Planning, 39,* 33–49. doi: 10.1075/lplp.39.1.02fai

Faingold, E. D. (2016a). Language rights for minorities and the right to code-switch in the United States. In P. C. Miller, B. G. Rubrecht, E. A. Mikulec, & C. T. McGivern (Eds.), *Readings in language studies, volume 6: A critical examination of language and community* (pp. 1–13). Grandville, MI: International Society for Language Studies.

Faingold, E. D. (2016b). Language rights in Catalonia and the constitutional right to secede from Spain. *Language Problems and Language Planning, 40,* 146–162. doi: 10.1075/lplp.40.2.02fai

Faingold, E. D. (2017). Language rights in the constitutions, organic acts, and statutes of the territories and associated states of the United States. *Language Problems and Language Planning, 41,* 103–114. doi: 10.1075/lplp.41.2.01fai

Fernández Asensio, R. (2014). Language policies in the Kingdom of Hawai'i: Reassessing linguicism. *Language Problems and Language Planning, 38,* 128–148. doi:10.1075/lplp.38.2.02fer

Fishman, J. A. (2006). Language policy and language shift. In T. Ricento (Ed.), *Language policy: Theory and method* (pp. 311–328). Malden, MA: Blackwell.

Fishman, J., Gertner, M., Lowy, E. G., & Milán, W. G. (1986). Preface: Language and culture, the ethnic revival and the sociolinguistic enterprise. In J. Fishman, M. Gertner, E. G. Lowy, & W. G. Milán (Eds.), *The rise and fall of the ethnic revival: Perspectives on language and ethnicity (Contributions to the sociology of language)* (pp. xi-xiv). Berlin, Germany: Mouton de Gruyter.

Flores, S. Y. and Murillo Jr., E. G. (2001). Power, language and ideology: Historical and contemporary notes on the dismantling of bilingual education. *The Urban Review, 33*, 183–206. doi: 10.1023/A:1010361803811

Freeman, L. D. (1975). The students' rights to their own language: Its legal bases. *College Composition and Communication, 26*, 25–29.

Gándara, P., & Orfield, G. (2012). Why Arizona matters: The historical, legal, and political contexts of Arizona's instructional policies and U.S. linguistic hegemony. *Language Policy, 11*, 7–19. doi:10.1007/s10993–011–9227–2

García Cantú, G. (1971). *Las invasiones norteamericanas en México*. Mexico, DF: Ediciones Era.

Garibova, J., & Asgarova, M. (2009). Language policy and legislation in post-Soviet Azerbaijan. *Language Problems and Language Planning, 33*, 191–217. doi: 10.1075/lplp.33.3.01gar

Genara Griego, R. J. (n.d.). Spanish: What the New Mexico Constitution says. Retrieved from http://www.nmhcpl.org/uploads/what_the_N_M_Constitution_says.pdf.

Glenn, E. N. (2002). *Unequal freedom: How race and gender shaped American citizenship and labor*. Cambridge, MA: Harvard University Press.

Gonzales, R. (2001). *Message to Aztlán: Selected writings*. Houston, Texas: Arte Público Press.

Grabowski, J. F., & Grabowski, P. A. (1992). *U.S. territories and possessions*. New York, NY: Chelsea House Publishers.

Green, D. W. (1986). Control, activation, and resource: A framework and model for the control of speech in bilinguals. *Brain and Language, 27*, 210–223. Available at: http://www.journals.elsevier.com/brain-and-language

Green, D. W. (1998). Mental control of the bilingual lexico-semantic system. *Bilingualism: Language and Cognition, 1*, 67–81. doi: 130.64.77.193

Green, D. W., & Abutalebi, J. (2013). Language control in bilinguals: The adaptive control hypothesis. *Journal of Cognitive Psychology, 25*, 515–530. doi: 10.1080/20445911.2013.796377

Griswold del Castillo, R. (1990). *The Treaty of Guadalupe Hidalgo: A legacy of conflict*. Norman, OK: University of Oklahoma Press.

Grosjean, F. (1982). *Life with two languages: An introduction to bilingualism*. Cambridge, MA: Harvard University Press.

Grosjean, F. (1997). Processing mixed language: Issues, findings, and models. In A. M. B. De Groot and J. F. Kroll (Eds.), *Tutorials in bilingualism: Psycholinguistic perspectives* (pp. 225–254). Mahwah, NJ: Lawrence Erlbaum.

Grosjean, F. (1998). Studying bilinguals: Methodological and conceptual issues. *Bilingualism, Language and Cognition, 1*, 131–149. doi: 10.1017/S136672899800025X

Grosjean, F. (2001). The bilingual's language modes. In J. Nicol (Ed.), *One mind, two languages: Bilingual language processing* (pp. 1–22). Oxford, UK: Blackwell.

Haney López, I. F. (2003). *Racism on trial: The Chicano fight for justice*. Cambridge, MA: Harvard University Press.

Haugen, E. (1956). *Bilingualism in the Americas: A bibliography and research guide*. Montgomery, AL: University of Alabama Press.

Hermans, D., Ormel, E., van Besselar, R., & van Hell, T. (2011). Lexical activation in bilinguals' speech is dynamic: How language ambiguous words can affect cross language activation. *Language and Cognitive Processes, 26*, 1687–1709. doi: 10.1080/01690965.2010.530411

Herriman, M., & Burnaby, B. (Eds.). (1996). *Language policies in English-dominant countries*. Clevedon, England: Multilingual Matters.

Hewitt-Robertson, D. J. (1992). *Oral language development in language rich multicultural kindergarten classrooms in Guam* (Unpublished doctoral dissertation). Texas Women University, Houston, TX.

Hezel, F. X. (1983). *The first taint to civilization: A history of the Caroline and the Marshall Islands in pre-colonial days*. Honolulu, HI: University of Hawaii Press.

Hogan, T. (2014). Flores v. Arizona. In S. C. K. Moore (Ed.), *Language policy processes and consequences* (pp. 28–44). Clevedon, UK: Multilingual Matters.

Holm, J. (1988). *Pidgins and creoles: Volume 1, Theory and structure*. Cambridge, UK: Cambridge University Press.

Huebner, T. (1984). Vernacular literacy, English as a language of wider communication, and language shift in American Samoa. *Journal of Multilingual and Multicultural Development, 7*, 393–411. doi: 10.1080/01434632.1986.9994255

Hunner, J. (2001). Preserving Hispanic lifeways in New Mexico. *The Public Historian, 23*, 29–40. doi: 10.1525/tph.2001.23.4.29

Huws, C. F. (2006). The Welsh language act 1993: A measure of success? *Language Policy, 5*, 141–160. doi: 10.1007/s10993–006–9000–0

Kilty, K. M. (2000). Racism, nativism, and exclusion: Public policy, immigration, and the Latino experience in the United States. *Journal of Poverty, 4*, 1–25. doi: 10.1300/j134v04n01_01

King, R. D. (1997). Should English be the Law? *The Atlantic*, April 1997. Retrieved from https://www.theatlantic.com/magazine/archive/1997/04/should-english-be-the-law/376825/

King, R. (1999). Lessons of public linguistics. *Southwest Journal of Linguistics, 18*, 1–14.

Krahnke, K., Hoffman, L., & Krahnke, K. (2003). Managing language use in the workplace. *The Journal of Behavioral and Applied Management, 4*, 148–157. Available at: https://jbam.scholasticahq.com/issue/276

Kriesi, H., & Trechsel, A. H. (2008). *The politics of Switzerland: Continuity and change in a consensus democracy*. Cambridge, UK: Cambridge University Press.

Kymlicka, W. (1995). *Multicultural citizenship*. Oxford, UK: Oxford University Press.

Labov, W. (1978). *Sociolinguistic patterns*. Oxford, UK: Blackwell.

Leckie, A. G., Kaplan, S. E., & Rubinstein-Avila, E. (2013). The need for speed: A critical discourse analysis of the reclassification of English language learners in Arizona. *Language Policy, 12*, 159–176. doi: 10.1007/s10993–012–9242-y

Leibowitz, A. H. (1989). *Defining status: A comprehensive analysis of U.S. territorial policy*. Dordrecht, the Netherlands: Martinus Nijhoff Publishers.

Lévesque, R. (1997). Accounts of early contact: Non-Spanish visitors to Guam before 1830. In L. D. Carter, W. L. Wuerch, & R. R. Carter (Eds.), *Guam history: Perspectives, volume 2*. (117–150). Mangilao, Guam: University of Guam.

Linder, W. (2010). *Swiss democracy: Possible solutions to conflict in multicultural societies*. Houndmills, Basingstoke, UK: Palgrave Macmillan.

Lipski, J. (1985). *Linguistic aspects of Spanish-English language switching*. Tempe, AZ: Center for Latin American Studies, Arizona State University.

López Tijerina, R. (2000). *They called me "King Tiger": My struggle for the land and our rights*. Houston, Texas: Arte Público Press.

Lutz, C. (2010). U.S. military bases on Guam in global perspective. *The Asia-Pacific Journal: Japan Focus, 8.30*, 1–21. Retrieved from http://apjjf.org/-Catherine-Lutz/3389/article.html

Mackey, W. E. (2010). *History and origins of language policies in Canada*. In M. A. Morris (Ed.), Canadian language policies in comparative perspective (pp. 18–66). Montreal, Canada: McGill-Queen's University Press.

MacLean. N. (2007). The Civil Rights Act and the transformation of Mexican American identity and politics. *Berkeley La Raza Law Journal, 18*, 123–134. doi: 10.15779/Z38237R

MacMillan, M. (1998). *The practice of language rights in Canada*. Toronto, Canada: University of Toronto Press.

MacSwan, J., & McAlister, K. T. (2010). Naturalistic and elicited data in grammatical studies of code-switching. *Studies in Hispanic and Lusophone Linguistics, 3,* 521–532. doi: 10.1515/shll20101085

Mangual Figueroa, A. (2013). Citizenship status and language education policy in an emerging Latino community in the United States. *Language Policy, 12,* 333–354. doi: 10.1007/s10993–013–9275-x

Mar-Molinero, C. (2000). The Iberian Peninsula: Conflicting linguistic nationalisms. In S. Barbour & C. Carmichael (Eds.), *Language and nationalism in Europe* (pp. 83–104). Oxford, UK: Oxford University Press.

Marin, C. (2016). *Papel Chicano dos: Works on paper from the collection of Cheech Marin.* San Diego, CA: Melissa Richardson Banks of CauseConnect, LLC.

Martinez, G. (2008). Language-in-healthcare policy, interaction patterns, and unequal care on the U.S.-Mexico border. *Language Policy, 7,* 345–363. doi: 10.1007/s10993–008–9110-y

Martinez. R. A. (2014). "Do they even know that they do it?" Exploring awareness of Spanish-English code-switching in a six-grade English language arts classroom. *Bilingual Research Journal, 37,* 195–210. doi: 10.180/15235882.2014.934972

Martinez-Brawley, E. E., & Zorita Paz, M. B. (2001). Latino immigrants in the borderlands: Transcultural lessons from the academy. *International Social Work, 44,* 55–73. doi: 10.1177/002087280104400106

May, S. (2000). Extending ethnolinguistic democracy in Europe: The case of Wales. *The Sociological Review, 48,* 147–172. doi: 10.1111/j.1467–954x.2000.tb03510.x

McKay, S., & Hornberger, N. (1996). *Sociolinguistics and language teaching.* Cambridge, UK: Cambridge University Press.

Meeks, E. V. (2007). *Border citizens: The making of indians, Mexicans, and Anglos in Arizona.* Austin, TX: University of Texas Press.

Monnig, L. A. (2007). *"Proving Chamorro": Indigenous narratives of race, identity, and decolonization of Guam* (Unpublished doctoral dissertation). University of Illinois, Urbana-Champaign, IL.

Mülhäusler, P. (1996). *Linguistic ecology: Language change and linguistic imperialism in the Pacific region.* London, UK: Routledge.

Myers-Scotton, C. (1990). Code-switching and borrowing: Interpersonal and macrolevel meaning. In R. Jacobson (Ed.), *Codeswitching as a worldwide phenomenon* (pp. 85–110). New York, NY: Peter Lang.

Myers-Scotton, C., & Jake, J. L. (2000). Matching lemmas in a bilingual language competence and production model: Evidence from intra-sentential code-switching. In L. Wei (Ed.), *The bilingual reader* (pp. 281–324). London, UK: Routledge.

Natividad, L. L., & Leon Guerrero, V. L. (2010). The explosive growth of U.S. military power on Guam confronts people power: Experience of an island people under Spanish, Japanese, and American colonial rule. *The Asia-Pacific Journal: Japan Focus, 8.49,* 1–20. Retrieved from http://apjjf.org/-LisaLinda-Natividad/3454/article.html

Palmer, D. (2009). Code-switching and symbolic power in a second grade two-way classroom: A teacher's motivation system gone awry. *Bilingual Research Journal, 32,* 42–59. doi: 10.1080/15235880902965854

Palmer, D., & Lynch, W. A. (2008). A bilingual education for a monolingual text? The pressure to prepare for TAKS and its influence on choices for language of instruction in Texas elementary bilingual classrooms. *Language Policy, 7,* 217–235. doi: 10.1007/s10993–008–9100–0

Palomo, R. S. (1987). American policies and practices affecting language shift on Guam: 1898 – 1950. In M. L. Spencer (Ed.), *Chamorro language issues and research on Guam: A book of readings* (pp. 19–43). Mangilao, GU: University of Guam.

Pesch, W. D. (1997). A history of Sanvitores in Guam, 1668 to 1672. In L. D. Carter, W. L. Wuerch, & R. R. Carter (Eds.), *Guam history: Perspectives, volume 1.* (67–94). Mangilao, GU: University of Guam.

Phillipson, R. (2003). *English-only Europe? Challenging language policy.* New York: Routledge.

Phillipson, R., & Skutnabb-Kangas, T. (1996). English-only worldwide or language ecology. *TESOL Quarterly, 30,* 429–452. doi: 10.2307/3587692

Pinker, S. (1994). *The language instinct.* New York, NY: Harper Collins.

Poplack, S. (2000). Sometimes I'll start in Spanish y termino en español: Toward a typology of code-switching. In L. Wei (Ed.), *The bilingual reader* (pp. 221–256). London, UK: Routledge.

Porterfield, J. (2006). *The Treaty of Guadalupe Hidalgo, 1848: A primary source of examination of the Treaty that ended the Mexican-American War.* New York, NY: The Rosen Publishing Group.

Reagan, T. (2004). Multilingualism in South Africa: "Dit is nou ons erns." *Language Problems and Language Planning, 28,* 107–111. doi: 10.1075/lplp.28.2.01rea

Rendon, A. B. (1971). *Chicano manifesto.* New York, NY: Collier Books.

Ricento, T. (1996). Language policy in the United States. In M. Herriman & B. Burnaby (Eds.), *Language policies in English-dominant countries* (pp. 122–158). Clevedon, England: Multilingual Matters.

Ridgell, R. (1997). Historical significance of Guam's geography. In L. D. Carter, W. L. Wuerch, & R. R. Carter (Eds.), *Guam history: Perspectives, volume 1.* (pp. 239–282). Mangilao, GU: University of Guam.

Riley, G. A. (1975). Language loyalty and ethnocentrism in the Guamanian speech community. *Anthropological Linguistics, 17,* 286–292. Retrieved from http://0-www.jstor.org.library.utulsa.edu/stable/pdf/30027443.pdf

Riley, G. A. (1980). Language loyalty and ethnocentrism in the Guamanian speech community: Seven years later. *Anthropological Linguistics, 22,* 329–333. Retrieved from http://0-www.jstor.org.library.utulsa.edu/stable/pdf/30027493.pdf

Robertson, M. (2001). Abridging the freedom of non-English speech: English-only legislation and the free speech rights of government employees. *Brigham Young University Law Review,* 2001, 641–696. Available at: http://digitalcommons.law.byu.edu/lawreview/vol2001/iss4/4

Rogers, R. F. (1995). *Destiny's landfall: A history of Guam.* Honolulu, HI: University of Hawai'i Press.

Sablan, V. A. (1997). *Teacher efficacy in the bilingual context of the Pacific island of Guam* (Unpublished doctoral dissertation). San Diego State University, San Diego, CA.

Sanchez, P. C. (1987). *Guam: The history of our island.* Agana, GU: Sanchez Publishing House.

San Miguel, Jr., G., & Valencia, R. (1998). From the Treaty of Guadalupe Hidalgo to Hopwood: The educational plight and struggle of Mexican Americans in the Southwest. *Harvard Educational Review, 68,* 353–412. Available at: http://hepg.org/her-home/issues/harvard-educational-review-volume-68-issue-3

Santos-Bamba, S. J. Q. (2013). The languages of three generations of Chamorro women. *Pacific Asia Inquiry, 4,* 84–93. Retrieved from http://www.uog.edu/sites/default/files/santos-bamba_languages-chamorro-women.pdf

Schiffman, H. F. (1996). *Linguistic culture and language policy.* London, UK: Routledge.

Schmidt, J. (2014). *The politics of English in Puerto Rico's public schools.* Boulder, CO: First Forum Press.

Schmitt, D. E. (1984). Ethnic minorities and the potential for violence and separatist activity: The cases of Northern Ireland and the Southwestern United States. *Current Research on Peace and Violence, 7,* 128–148. Retrieved from http://www.jstor.org/stable/40724979

Shaffer, J. R. (2000). *American Sāmoa: 100 years under the United States flag.* Honolulu: HI: Island Heritage Publishing.

Shohamy, E. G. (2006). *Language policy: Hidden agendas and new approaches.* New York, NY: Routledge.

Sinsheimer, A. (2005). "English only" and our struggle to understand the concept of language. *Language and Communication, 25,* 61–80. doi: 10.1016/j.langcom.2004.04.003

Song, J. J. (2011). English as an official language in South Korea: Global English or social malady? *Language Problems and Language Planning, 35,* 35–55. doi: 10.1075/lplp.35.1.03son

Sperling, J. (2009). Improving immigrants' access to public services in the United States: Language access policy and policy implementation. *Current Issues in Language Planning, 10,* 405–421. doi: 10.1080/14664200903555013

Thomas, M. D. (2007, July). A shifting burden: Recent developments related to English-only policies in the workplace. *Employment Law Commentary.* Retrieved from http://media.mofo.com/docs/pdf/ELC0707.pdf.

Thompson, L. (1947). *Guam and its people.* Princeton, NJ: Princeton University Press.

Toribio, J. (2001a). Accessing bilingual code-switching competence. *International Journal of Bilingualism, 5,* 403–436. doi: 10.117/13670069010050040201

Toribio, J. (2001b). On the emergence of bilingual code-switching competence. *Bilingualism: Language and Cognition, 4,* 203–231. doi: 10.1017/S1366728901000414

Torres González, R. (2002). *Idioma, bilingüismo y nacionalidad: La presencia del inglés en Puerto Rico.* San Juan, PR: Editorial de la Universidad de Puerto Rico.

Tree, M. (2013). Catalan language literature: What's going on? In L. Castro (Ed.), *What's up with Catalonia* (pp. 147–152). Ashfield, MA: Catalonia Press.

Tucker, G. R. (2005). Innovative language education programs for heritage language students: The especial case of Puerto Ricans. *International Journal of Bilingual Education and Bilingualism, 8,* 188–205. doi: 10.1080/13670050508668606

Tully, J. (1995). *Strange multiplicity: Constitutionalism in an age of diversity.* Cambridge, UK: Cambridge University Press.

Turi, G. (1994). Typology of language legislation. In T. Skutnabb-Kangas & R. Phillipson (Eds.), *Linguistic human rights: Overcoming linguistic discrimination* (pp. 111–119). Berlin, Germany: Mouton de Gruyter.

Underwood, R. A. (1987). *American education and the acculturation of the Chamorros of Guam* (Unpublished doctoral dissertation) University of Southern California, Los Angeles, CA.

U.S. Census. (2010). Retrieved from http://factfinder2.census.gov/faces/tableservices/jsf/pages/productview.xhtml?pid=DEC_10_SF1_GCTP3.US04PR&prodType=table

Valencia, R. R. (2008). *Chicano students and the courts: The Mexican American legal struggle for education equality.* New York, NY: New York University Press.

Varennes, F. de. (1996). *Language, minorities and human rights.* Leiden, Netherlands: Martinus Nijhoff.

Vélez, J. (2000). Understanding Spanish-language maintenance in Puerto Rico: Political will meets the demographic imperative. *International Journal of the Sociology of Language, 142,* 5–24. doi: 10.1515/ijsl.2000.142.5

Veltman, C. (1983). *Languages shift in the United States.* Berlin, Germany: Mouton.

Veltman, C. (1988). *The future of the Spanish language in the United States.* New York & Washington DC: Hispanic Policy Development Project.

Wallace, B. (1964). English language teaching in Samoa. *Language Learning, 14,* 167–172. doi: 10.1111/j.1467–1770.1964.tb01304.x

Weber, D. J. (2003). *Foreigners in their native land: Historical roots of the Mexican Americans.* Albuquerque, NM: University of New Mexico Press.

Willens, H. P., & Siemer, D. C. (2002). *An honorable accord: The covenant between the Northern Mariana Islands and the United States.* Honolulu, HI: University of Hawai'i Press.

Williams, C. H. (2008). *Linguistic minorities in democratic context.* Houndmills, Basingstoke, UK: Palgrave Macmillan.

Wilson Moore, S. A. (2003). "We feel the want of protection": The politics of law and race in California, 1848 – 1878. *California History,* 81, 96–125. doi: 10.2307/25161701

Wiseman, N. (2010). The quest for a Quebec constitution. *American Review of Canadian Studies, 40,* 56–70. doi: 10.1080/02722010903545194

Wright, S. (1999) (Ed.). *Language, democracy, and devolution in Catalonia.* Clevedon, UK: Multilingual Matters.

Zentella, A. C. (1997). *Growing up bilingual: Puerto Rican children in New York.* Malden, MA: Blackwell.

Zuckerman, M. (2010). Constitutional clash: When English-only meets voting rights. *Yale Law & Policy Review, 28,* 353–377. Available at: http://digitalcommons.law.yale.edu/ylpr/vol28/iss2/5

Index

About the Author

Eduardo D. Faingold is professor of Spanish and linguistics at the University of Tulsa and holds a Ph.D. in Linguistics from Tel-Aviv University. Faingold has held visiting appointments at the University of California Los Angeles, Stony Brook University, New York University, the University of Cape Town, the Hebrew University of Jerusalem, Tel-Aviv University, the Technical University of Berlin, and the Max Planck Institute, and received numerous grants and fellowships from the National Endowment for the Humanities, the German Science Foundation, the German Academic Exchange Service (DAAD), the South African Science Foundation, the Hebrew University of Jerusalem, Tel-Aviv University, and the University of Tulsa. He is the author of numerous articles in prestigious refereed journals such as *Language Problems and Language Planning, International Journal of Jewish Education Research, Journal of Pidgin and Creole Languages, Estudios de Lingüística Aplicada, International Journal of Bilingual Education and Bilingualism, Journal of Psycholinguistic Research,* and *Language Sciences*, as well as books published by academic publishers such as Palgrave Macmillan, Rowman & Littlefield, and Gunter Narr Verlag, in applied linguistics, psycholinguistics, bilingualism, immigration studies, and language policy.

CPSIA information can be obtained
at www.ICGtesting.com
Printed in the USA
LVHW090509290620
659254LV00007B/31

9 781498 571364